DIEPPE
THROUGH THE LENS
OF THE
GERMAN WAR PHOTOGRAPHER

Text: HUGH G. HENRY Jr
Photos: JEAN PAUL PALLUD

AFTER THE
BATTLE

Credits

© Hugh G. Henry Jr/*After the Battle*
ISBN: 0 900913 76 2
Printed in Great Britain
Designed by Winston G. Ramsey, Editor *After the Battle*

PUBLISHERS
Battle of Britain Prints International Limited
Church House, Church Street, London E15 3JA

PRINTERS
Plaistow Press Limited,
Church House, Church Street, London E15 3JA

PHOTOGRAPHS
Bundesarchiv, Postfach 320, 5400 Koblenz, Germany
Cover, centre 291/1905/13A, *Page 14* 291/1209/16A, *14, inset left* 291/1209/32, *17* 362/2207/34, *18* MW6379/32A, *19* MW6379/34A, *20* MW6379/38A, *27* 362/2209/14, *28* 362/2208/10A, *29 inset* 291/1205/35A, *32* MW6380/18A, *33* 362/2207/15, *34* 291/1905/13A, *35* 362/2207/22, *36* 362/2207/13, *38* 362/2207/36, *40* 291/1242/6, *41* 362/2207/37, *44* 362/2211/4, *56* 362/2211/3, *57* 362/2211/2, *63* MW6380/6A, *Rear endpaper left* 291/1242/12

ECP Armées, Fort D'Ivry, 94205 Ivry sur Seine, Cedex, Paris, France
Front endpaper right DAA 2811 L06, *Cover, top left* DAM 1132 L16, *Cover, top right* DAM 1142 L20, *Cover, bottom left* DAA 2815 L3, *Cover, bottom right* DAA 2815 L02, *Page 1* DAA 2813 L13, *13* DAA 2815 L28, *14, inset right* DAT 2126 L33, *16* DAA 2815 L14, *19, inset* DAM 1135 L23, *21* DAA 2815 L25, *22* DAA 2813 L15, *23, left* DAM 1140 L20, *23, right* DAM 1141 L09, *24* DAT 2126 L09, *25* DAA 2813 L08, *26* DAA 2815 L09, *29* DAA 2815 L04, *30* DAA 2813 L09, *31* DAT 2126 L32, *37* DAM 1142 L27, *39* DAT 2126 L44, *42* DAA 2815 L01, *43* DAM 1142 L29, *45* DAT 2126 L08, *46* DAT 2126 L25, *47* DAA 2813 L10, *48* DAM 1141 L13, *49* DAT 2126 L11, *50* DAM 1137 L04, *51* DAM 1132 L02, *52* DAM 1137 L18, *53* DAA 2815 L18, *54* DAM 1137 L22, *55, left* DAT 2126 L36, *58* DAT 2126 L07, *59* DAM 1132 L18, *60 top left* CTT 10 262, *bottom right* DAA 2812 L4, *61* DAT 2132 L10, *62* DAM 1142 L8, *64* DAT 2162 L13, *Back cover* DAT 2134 L12, *Rear endpaper right* DAT 2126 L41

National Archives of Canada, 395 Wellington Street, Ottawa, Ontario K1A ON3, Canada
Front endpaper left PMR 93-040, *Page 3, top left* C 138677, *3, bottom right* C 138694, *5, top left* C 138692, *5, bottom right* C 138686, *6, top left* C 138680, *6, top right* C 138681, *7, top left* C 138689, *7, top right* C 138690, *8* C 138688

Imperial War Museum, Lambeth Road, London SE1 6HZ
Page 4 H20178, *9* A11231

Air Photo Library, Keele University, Keele, Staffordshire, ST5 5BG
Pages 10-11 C/257 519/574

Studio Henry IV, 26 Rue de la Boucherie, 76200 Dieppe, France
Page 55, right

ENDPAPERS: *Front left:* **Preparing for battle. Men of The Calgary Regiment prepare the light armament of their Churchill AMOS at Seaford, Sussex on May 5, 1942. L–R: Trooper Jack Haase, Sergeant Jim V. Batchelor (crew commander), Troopers W. A. Johnston, J. F. 'Frank' Cadden, of 1 Troop A Squadron and, standing on the right, 1 Troop Leader Lieutenant Chester J. Macdonald. The fifth man of the crew at the back cannot be identified. In the event, this troop failed to get ashore.** *Front right:* **The only street in Dieppe with an access gate from the promenade into the town was the Rue de Sygogne.** *Rear left:* **The aftermath. The victors prepare to winch BLUEBELL from the sea.** *Rear right:* **The real cost of battle; 22-year-old Captain Douglas G. Purdy from BULL of 8 Troop B Squadron now rests in peace in the Canadian War Cemetery at Dieppe.**

Dedication

This book is dedicated to all men of The Calgary Regiment (Tank) who served their country during the Second World War, especially to those members who participated in the Dieppe operation and became prisoners-of-war — Onward Calgary Tanks!

Acknowledgements

The text for this work is a revised extract from the author's Master of Arts dissertation *The Tanks at Dieppe: The 14th Canadian Army Tank Regiment (The Calgary Regiment [Tank]), 1939 — 19 August 1942* completed in July 1991 at the University of Victoria, British Columbia, Canada. Sources of information, aside from the usual secondary ones such as the British and Canadian official histories, memoirs and relevant standard monographs, include such primary material as the regimental war diary, intelligence reports, battle narratives, operation orders, German reports, battle maps, and photographs. The majority of documents were obtained from The King's Own Calgary Regiment Archives, Calgary; the Directorate of History, National Defence Headquarters, Ottawa; the National Archives of Canada, Ottawa; and the Public Record Office, Kew, London. Finally, interviews and correspondence with many veterans of the regiment clarified details and gave insights into areas not covered by the written records.

I would like to express thanks to several individuals and, in general, to the 50/14 Veterans' Association, Calgary, without whose support this book would not have been possible. I am indebted to my supervisor, Professor Reginald H. Roy, who originally suggested the topic as part of my Master of Arts dissertation, and who maintained my focus on the topic when I tended to deviate. Credit must go to the other three members of my examining committee, Professors Patricia Roy, Michael Hadley and David Zimmerman, who were able to give me constructive criticism on the many preliminary drafts.

Special mention must go to Lieutenant-Colonel R. G. 'Dick' Maltby, who constantly gave me enthusiastic support in this endeavour, reading preliminary drafts, giving suggestions and putting me in touch with other veterans. Other individuals who deserve credit are Brigadier C. A. 'Stoney' Richardson, Lieutenant-Colonel Alex F. McIntosh, Lieutenant-Colonel C. R. 'Bob' Sharp, Captain Gordon L. Drysdale, Captain Ian R. Seymour, Captain Edwin Bennett, Lieutenant Jack H. Dunlap, Stan A. Kanik, and other veterans of the regiment with whom I was in contact. I would like to express thanks to Bob Wyman and Jack Jenner who let me have free access to the private diaries, letters, personal papers and scrapbooks of their fathers. Thanks is also owed to Dr W. A. B. Douglas and his staff at the Directorate of History and Denise Ross and the staff of the National Archives, who were always helpful and efficient in quickly processing my numerous requests for information. Finally, I am grateful to my parents and close friends, Catherine Foskett and Ian Q. R. Thomas, who have unwaveringly supported me during my academic training.

HUGH G. HENRY Jr, M.A.

Abbreviations

ALO	Air (Intelligence) Liaison Officer		**PBM**	Principal Beach Master
AMLO(T)	Assistant Military Landing Officer (Tank)		**PMLO**	Principal Military Landing Officer
			PRU	Photo Reconnaissance Unit (RAF)
ASSU	Air Support Signals Unit		**RAF**	Royal Air Force
CAC	Canadian Armoured Corps		**RANVR**	Royal Australian Naval Volunteer Reserve
CATB	Canadian Army Tank Brigade			
CATR	Canadian Army Tank Regiment		**RCCS**	Royal Canadian Corps of Signals
COHQ	Combined Operations Headquarters		**RCE**	Royal Canadian Engineers
LCA	Landing Craft Assault		**SAMLO(T)**	Senior Assistant Military Landing Officer (Tank)
LCP(L)	Landing Craft Personnel (Large)			
OR	Other Ranks		**TLC**	Tank Landing Craft

Introduction

Since 1942, the Dieppe Raid has been the subject of much controversy surrounding its political and military background, aims, plans, execution and supposed 'lessons learned'. Although historians have documented their arguments well, they have not examined accurately or in any detail the operations of The Calgary Regiment (Tank), 14th Canadian Army Tank Regiment (14 CATR), Canadian Armoured Corps. Some misunderstandings and myths concerning the tanks and men, their performance and conditions affecting their actions, must be dispelled. At this point, it is worth noting that not only was the 14 CATR the first Canadian armoured unit ever to go into action, it was the first time in history that tanks were used in an amphibious landing, as well as the baptism of fire for the latest British equipment, such as the Tank Landing Craft (TLC) (later in the war amended to Landing Craft Tank — LCT), the new Churchill tank and its 6-pounder gun.

In early 1941, The Calgary Regiment (Tank) was mobilised as part of the newly-formed 1st Canadian Army Tank Brigade (1 CATB) and after only a few months of extremely basic training, first with no vehicles or modern equipment and later with Great War vintage, American-maufactured Renault tanks, the complete 1 CATB was sent overseas. It was to join the rest of the Canadian Army Overseas which formed the backbone of Great Britain's defence against the expected German invasion. During the remainder of the year, besides the normal training of driving and maintenance of tanks, wireless instruction, map-reading, range firing, reconnaissance and tactical training were carried out. In the Spring of 1942 several Canadian divisional and corps anti-invasion exercises, code-named 'Beaver', were carried out in the open country of southern England. During 'Beaver III', the 14 CATR performed the most satisfactorily of all armoured units and therefore was chosen for the Dieppe operation. The reason the regiment always did so well on exercises was simply because of regimental spirit and superior skills. The majority of men were from small farming towns around Calgary and already knew each other, leading to strong unit cohesion. As farmers, they were more skilled and experienced in handling many types of heavy machinery, often similar to driving a tank, than most men in the eastern regiments and thus were ahead of them in related training.

In mid-May, the 14 CATR moved to the Isle of Wight and undertook one month of experimental waterproofing of tanks that required much improvisation and testing and practised loading and unloading tanks from the TLCs. Several amphibious exercises, and two rehearsals in the area of Bridport on the Dorset coast, were carried out with engineers and infantry of the 2nd Canadian Division to give the tank crews experience in supporting other ground units assaulting a defended beach. Unfortunately none of the beaches had towns fronting them or the same stony beaches as at Dieppe. A typical exercise began by securing a beach-head, then moving a few miles inland over open country to capture an objective, such as an airport, and finally covering the withdrawal of the infantry to the beach before the tanks re-embarked themselves. The regiment never underwent street-fighting training in any villages or towns. In the middle of August the regiment was ordered to prepare for another amphibious assault scheme. All tanks, vehicles, ammunition, and personnel were loaded on the TLCs at Gosport and Newhaven by August 18, at which time the men were informed that the exercise would be an actual operation against Dieppe.

The plan originated in early April 1942 at Combined Operations Headquarters (COHQ) under the command of Vice-Admiral Lord Louis Mountbatten, and was part of a series of raids, of ever-increasing size and intensity, designed to gain experience in amphibious operations, and test new techniques and equipment for the future invasion of the Continent. At the time, capturing a port in usable condition was a fundamental and unchangeable determinate in all invasion planning. COHQ planners chose Dieppe in this context and because they judged it had adequate defences to test a divisional-size assault while still being within the necessary range of fighter cover. The operation, code-named 'Rutter', originally scheduled for June 20-21, 1942, was postponed several times in early July and was indefinitely cancelled on July 7 due to unfavourable weather conditions. The decision to revive the raid about a week later, redesignated 'Jubilee', and the exact status of its authorisation continues to be controversial. A serious deficiency in the plan was the

Two of the actual vehicles which participated in the Dieppe landing pictured during training. We shall see both the Churchill I *(top left)*, **named BOLSTER (T31107R), and Jeep CM4218884** *(above)* **lying abandoned on the beach later on.**

Thorness Bay on the Isle of Wight in May 1942. Two beach assault engineers reverse a Caterpillar D7 angle-dozer onto a TLC during disembarking training. None of the bulldozers managed to get ashore during the raid. In the background is *TLC No. 121*, later redesignated *TLC-5* [6], which was one of the three derelict TLCs on the beach at Dieppe.

During July 1942, on a beach near Seaford, Sussex, the 14 CATR trained in scaling sea-walls up to seven feet high with the aid of timber crib ramps. Under favourable conditions, a highly trained squad of 30 beach assault engineers could construct a ramp in five minutes. For these tests the materials were carried a distance of 30 yards and consisted of thirty 6in.×12in.×12ft timbers and eight 12in.×12in.×4ft chocks weighing approximately five tons. Twelve-foot vehicle bridge ramps, together with timber ramps, were used on high walls and directly on low walls for wheeled vehicles. The Churchill pictured is from C Squadron Headquarters F Troop.

cancellation of a preliminary heavy naval and air bombardment and the lack of heavy naval support artillery. Instead, four Hunt class destroyers, with only 4.7-inch guns, were to briefly bombard, for about ten minutes, the buildings and frontal installations at Dieppe before switching their fire to the headlands on either side of the town where the Germans had emplaced heavy coastal guns. Similarly, Air Marshal Sir Charles Portal, Chief of the Air Staff, refused to risk losing bombers needed for the strategic bombing of Germany. So the heavy air bombardment component was dropped.

Another significant fault in the plan, probably the result of the COHQ planners' attempt to maintain secrecy, was they did not inform or request the assistance of the Air (Intelligence) Liaison Officers (ALOs) and Army Co-op Command, the organisation specialising in ground/air co-operation. No ALOs went with the fighter squadrons which carried out the low-level attacks. No Air Support Signals Unit (ASSU) tentacles were arranged forward with the infantry and tank units on the beaches and backwards to the fighter headquarters and airfields in Britain. Finally, Army Co-op Command sent out 72 low-level reconnaissances, using the new American Mustang single-seater fighter, losing ten of them, for no reason, since they had no direct radio links with the forward ground units or naval support vessels.

An important consideration during the planning was where to land the tanks. Since all planners agreed that rivers had to be avoided, the tanks could only land between the mouths of the Scie and Arques rivers — this meant either on the beach at Dieppe or a small part of the beach at Pourville, two miles to the west. In an appreciation of the

outline plan for 'Jubilee' by the 2nd Canadian Division, General Staff Officer 1, Lieutenant-Colonel Churchill C. Mann, naïvely pointed out that tanks assaulting Dieppe could give immediate fire support to the attacking infantry and engineers and cause a psychological shock to the Germans and civilian population. Ammunition and engineer support material for tanks could be supplied more easily on the main beach where the supply craft concentration point was. The tanks would also be closer to their planned objectives and the beach front was the most convenient place for re-embarkation after the raid.

Lieutenant-Colonel Mann recognised the disadvantages of attacking the enemy frontally, the need for engineer assault teams, and the difficulty of penetrating blocked streets due to bombardment, but he pointed out that the garrison only consisted of two low-grade infantry companies. Opting in favour of the plan, he concluded that the tanks would play an important part in the withdrawal phase and that, in general, the tanks 'seemed to have a reasonable prospect of success'.

The idea of trying to send a tank cavalry charge through the narrow streets of an enemy defended town, and out into the surrounding countryside, holding a defensive perimeter and then withdrawing through the town, all in the matter of five and a half hours, was ridiculously foolhardy and reckless. It also showed gross ignorance on the part of COHQ planners and senior Allied commanders of the capabilities and limitations of tanks. No one seems to have considered the extreme vulnerability of tanks taking part in street fighting in built-up areas. Vision from a tank is considerably impaired. If a crew commander stuck his head out of the turret to get a clear view, he was exposed to enemy sniper fire. Tanks could neither protect themselves nor return fire unless at some distance from the target because their guns could not be elevated very high. Also because they depended on the infantry, they moved slowly.

ROUNDER, of Regimental Headquarters, is pictured here most probably during a 'Yukon' assault landing exercise in June 1942. No problem was found in breaching the 2in. tubular scaffolding beach defences. ROUNDER did not land during Operation 'Jubilee'.

THE ASSAULT PLAN AND INTELLIGENCE

The assault would be on a front of approximately ten miles at five different points. At 0450 hours precisely, after the short naval bombardment and air attack by cannon equipped Hurricanes and Spitfires, the surprise flank attacks would go in, followed half an hour later by the main assault on the town. In all, 60 RAF and Allied Air Forces' squadrons were involved in the largest single air battle of the war over the Dieppe area. The Allied Air Forces lost 106 aircraft while the Germans had 48 destroyed. Effective air cover for the ground units was not possible because the operational conditions dictated its nature and scope. The flight from southern England to Dieppe used most of the fighters' fuel, leaving them only about ten minutes flying time over the area before they had to return. The German fighters could remain aloft much longer and had their airfields close by. Some Dieppe veterans, not realising these facts, have held a misplaced bitterness towards the RAF ever since the raid.

On the flanks, Commandos would capture and destroy the coastal batteries about five miles east and west of Dieppe, while infantry were to neutralise coastal batteries on the east and west headlands which dominated the town. The Cameron Highlanders of Canada were to advance to meet the tanks of A Squadron, 14 CATR, behind the town and then advance against another coastal battery, an emergency fighter airfield, and the local enemy divisional headquarters thought to be at Arques-la-Bataille. These flank attacks were an essential requirement for the success of the main frontal assault, half an hour later, and to ensure the safety of the naval support vessels. They were, in general, a failure.

The main attack was to capture the town and hold it for a limited period while demolitions were carried out. The beach was divided in half, the eastern (Red Beach) being invaded by the Essex Scottish Regiment, commanded by Lieutenant-Colonel Frederick K. Jasperson, while the western half (White Beach) was attacked by the Royal Hamilton Light Infantry, commanded by Lieutenant-Colonel Robert R. Labatt. Both regiments were to be supported by 58 tanks of the 14 CATR. Les Fusiliers Mont-Royal and 'A' Commando of the Royal Marines were to be held in reserve.

On June 11–12 and 22–23, 1942, all units designated for the Dieppe Raid took part in Exercise 'Yukon' I and II which were in fact rehearsals for the operation. These landings were on the coast of Dorset in the vicinity of West Bay and Bridport. The first exercise was a shambles, due mostly to naval errors, resulting in many units landing at the wrong beaches, late, or not at all. The TLCs themselves were over an hour late. The exercise showed the need for better liaison between all arms, improved wireless communications among all units, and more effective smoke cover from the air and sea. 'Yukon II' was more successful and therefore it was judged suitable to proceed with the raid, although the naval units still had some navigational problems to work out. A typical exercise involving the TLCs, as shown here, began with four-man squads of beach assault engineers, carried in the first flight of TLCs, running out ahead of the tanks to lay chespaling tracks.

The Canadian commanders, Lieutenant-General Andrew G. L. McNaughton, Commander-in-Chief First Canadian Army, Lieutenant-General Harry D. G. Crerar, commanding 1st Canadian Corps, and Major-General John H. 'Ham' Roberts, commanding 2nd Canadian Division, formally approved the final military plan by August 14. Even though any one of them could have vetoed it, this was probably out of the question since they would have been immediately castigated by their fellow officers who all wanted to see action; it would have been bad for the troops' morale and, besides, all three were confident in the operation's success.

In planning 'Jubilee', COHQ relied on imperfect intelligence. Sir F. H. Hinsley, the official historian of British intelligence during the Second World War, writes that COHQ planners were 'over-reliant on one source' of intelligence, photo reconnaissance, and 'took at face value' intelligence that underestimated the strength of the defences and the terrain. Shots taken from high elevations did not effectively show any defences hidden by building roofs or caves blasted into the cliffs of the headlands.

Given the limitations of photographic intelligence, it is regrettable that intelligence officers did not make a more careful evaluation of known defensive positions from the perspective of established German tactical doctrine. If COHQ had used its knowledge of the enemy order of battle and equipment in use, it could have made a more realistic and

The bundles weighed about 250lbs, were approximately 25 feet long and could be wired together to form a continuous track. These tracks could be moved around by the engineers to suit the later flights of incoming TLCs. All tanks, carriers and Jeeps then passed over these tracks, only becoming bogged down if they swerved off them. Since many of the scout cars had experienced difficulty even on the chespaling, it was decided that in future these should be towed ashore by the tanks. Note that the pebbles here are small, up to 2in. in diameter, whereas at Dieppe they are up to 6in. *Above:* **A Churchill Mark I exits (note the 3in. close support howitzer), followed by CANNY of 15 Troop, C Squadron, and scout car HECTOR. The latter two vehicles both landed at Dieppe. *TLC No. 303,* designated *TLC-13* for the operation, and carrying Major R. R. 'Black Bob' Taylor and A Squadron Headquarters F Troop, did not touch down on the beach.**

detailed evaluation of the defences on the beaches and in the cliffs. In actual fact, Dieppe had been turned into a fortress. The defences were sited in an 'anti-raid' rôle as opposed to an anti-invasion rôle meaning that the majority of the firepower was concentrated to cover the beaches.

The garrison consisted of two battalions and staff of the 571st Infantry Regiment amounting to approximately 1,500 men. The east and west headlands and cliffs contained numerous positions ideal for defence. Artillery, machine gun nests, and dual-purpose flak batteries were all sited to bring enfilade fire on the beach, while being cleverly hidden in depressions, caves and camouflaged bunkers. Allied Intelligence and COHQ planners underestimated the numbers and calibre of many of these guns.

The defences in town itself consisted of 37mm, 47mm and French 75mm anti-tank guns and heavy machine guns hidden in buildings fronting the promenade. They could fire directly into approaching landing craft. The 1,500-yard promenade was interspersed with concrete pillboxes siting similar weapons. Many of these emplacements had connecting trenches to open weapon pits from which German soldiers could hurl grenades at the crouching troops beside the sea-wall. Finally, the Germans had mortars precisely ranged on the beach. Lieutenant-Colonel Labatt in an after-action report stated that 'stakes for ranging were still standing on the beach from a mortar practice carried out the previous day. Their fire plan was well laid out and beautifully co-ordinated.'

THE CHERT BEACH, ENGINEERS AND TANK GADGETRY

A major intelligence blunder was the failure to identify the composition of the beach at Dieppe which proved to be the main technical difficulty for the tanks. The whole beach is composed of chert rocks which average one to six inches in diameter. Stan A. Kanik, a former trooper of A Squadron who was on the raid but did not land, returned to Dieppe several times after the war, most recently in 1992. Drawing on his knowledge as a geological engineer, his analysis of the beach clearly explains why many tanks had difficulty manoeuvring on the beach. He notes: 'the white cliffs are composed of siliceous chalk, interspersed with chert lenses and beds.' The chalk is easily dissolved and leaves behind the chert which under beach erosion is 'shaped into rounded and oblong stones (rocks) that resist cracking or breaking.' He continues, 'the entire beach is composed of chert stones, boulders and rubble,' which after tidal action, 'eventually rest at an "angle of repose" of about 15 to 20 degrees. Secondly, these rocks will extend many metres in depth, so vehicles cannot dig down to a solid rock base for traction. When a tracked or wheeled vehicle tries to climb up this slope, it immediately digs itself down; when the tracks are turned to either side the stones roll in between the drive sprocket and track and the object that first gives way is the pins holding the track links.'

All regimental and standard histories referring to Dieppe claim its beach is composed of 'shale' or 'pebbles.' The Allies had carried out landing tests with the tanks on the firm, sandy beaches of the Isle of Wight and on the small, pebbly beaches of Dorset, but not on a chert beach, such as found at Dover. The Germans, who had many such trials, found their tanks became bellied down and stuck and did not site any heavy anti-tank guns or place anti-tank mines on the beach in front of the town since they thought the beaches were not negotiable by tanks.

One supposed tank obstacle for which COHQ had planned was the sea-wall which the Royal Canadian Engineers (RCE) were to aid the tanks in crossing. The RCE were divided into two main groups — the Beach Assault Party (under Major B. Sucharov) and the Demolition Party (under Lieutenant-Colonel L. F. Barnes) and then sub-divided into various-sized squads depending on their tasks and distributed throughout the TLCs.

The Beach Assault Party was responsible for getting all troops, stores, tanks and other vehicles from the point of touchdown by the naval craft onto, across, and clear of the beach area. This meant demolishing any anti-tank concrete road blocks at the exits of the promenade and, using bulldozers to clear boulders, prepare ramps for evacuation and generally keep the beaches clear. If needed, these machines could also aid vehicles stuck on the beach and push off grounded landing craft. Ensuring that the tanks crossed over the sea-wall was the most important task of the Beach Assault Party. The sea-wall was

The complete 14 CATR on parade before participating in 'Yukon II'. In the foreground is COUGAR, 13 Troop, C Squadron, which we will see later immobilised on Dieppe's promenade. For this exercise, all the tanks had been waterproofed. Lieutenant R. G. 'Dick' Maltby recalls that: 'The practical work was carried out on the Isle of Wight using a school's swimming pool for dunking these 40-ton monsters. On one occasion, Generals Montgomery, McNaughton and Roberts witnessed the unsuccessful attempt to submerge a Churchill in 6 to 8 feet of water without killing the motor. The senior generals insisted on getting into the tank for the trial and wound up getting thoroughly soaked.'

estimated to be up to six feet in height. The 'Rutter' plan of using sappers to blow gaps in the wall had been dropped in favour of building timber crib ramps beside it for the tanks to climb. Under favourable conditions a highly-trained detachment of thirty engineers could carry the five tons of material neccessary thirty yards and build a ramp beside a seven-foot wall in five minutes. Due to the intensity of German firing, no timbers were ever unloaded.

Major Sucharov was assigned to develop a device to enable the tanks to get over the sea-wall. He came up with a carpet-laying device using chespaling, a flexible roll of chestnut fencing. An apparatus was designed to hold one roll of chespaling, three feet wide (the width of one track was 22 inches) and about 25 to 30 feet long in front of each track. Controlled electrically from the turret, the ends of the rolls could be released when the tank was the appropriate distance from the sea-wall. The rolls would then be gradually dragged under the tank's tracks. The tank could then mount up to a 28-inch wall without problem. After use, the whole apparatus could be jettisoned by an explosive charge, electrically set off from inside the turret. Finally, the Beach Assault Party was responsible for preparing for the successful reembarkation of all tanks and vehicles.

The Demolition Party was charged with demolishing power stations, petrol dumps, dockyard, dry-docks, swing bridges, gasworks, pumping stations, telephone exchanges and rail facilities. The group was split up into many small squads, each with its own commanding officer, and assigned precise objectives to be sabotaged once the infantry and tanks secured a perimeter around the town. Most of these squads never got off the beach. Indeed, the engineers had about 85 to 90 per cent casualties — the highest rate in the raid.

The tanks themselves had been adapted for amphibious operations up to a depth of six feet using rubber balloon fabric. Tall, box-shaped ducts (known as louvre extensions) were fitted to the air intake vents and the exhaust pipes were extended so as to be well above the water line. The waterproofing and the louvre extensions could be blown off by electrically-triggered cordite charges placed underneath them. The waterproofing procedure was still in the experimental stage and had never been tested under battle conditions. Such then were the plans and preparations of COHQ and the regiments involved. No contingency plans for failure existed so success now depended on the individuals of the assaulting force.

THE ATTACK BEGINS

Thirty minutes prior to the TLC's touchdown, the tanks were to start warming up their engines. Two types of TLCs were used and could hold three or four tanks and one or two smaller vehicles. Radio silence was maintained until zero hour. On the run in, mortar detachments of the Black Watch (Royal Highland Regiment) of Canada, located in the rear of two of the first TLCs lobbed 3-inch smoke bombs onto the promenade to add to the smoke-screen already supplied by the Royal Air Force. The infantry were to land first, followed immediately by the TLCs carrying the engineers and tanks which would give immediate supporting fire. C. P. Stacey, the official historian of the Canadian Army in the Second World War, points out: 'In any opposed landing, the first minute or two after the craft touch down are of crucial importance; and it may be said that during that minute or two the Dieppe battle, on the main beaches, was lost. The impetus of the attack ebbed quickly away, and by the time the tanks arrived the psychological moment was past.'

The first wave of tanks of the 14 CATR arrived about ten minutes late due to navigational error. During this critical period, the infantry had no fire support and the German defenders were able to recover from the short preliminary air and naval bombardment and man their weapons. Thus, the assaulting infantry were caught trying to blast gaps in the unexpectedly strong rows of wire, the majority becoming pinned down at the sea-wall, unable to dig slit trenches in the rocks. The Essex Scottish tried three times to cross the promenade but were repulsed each time with heavy casualties. Thereafter, they could only return fire from the limited protection of the sea-wall. By about 0630 hours, only an hour or so after landing, they had suffered at least 75 per cent casualties.

On White Beach, the Royal Hamilton Light Infantry were initially held up by the strongly fortified Casino. After stiff fighting, they cleared it despite many casualties. From the Casino they gave covering fire to some small groups attempting to penetrate the town. These units engaged in minor house-to-house and street fighting incidents with German patrols until they started to run out of ammunition. When they attempted to withdraw to the Casino, some were taken prisoner in the process. The infantry, initially pinned down behind the rows of barbed wire and sea-wall, were only able to pass these obstacles and later take the Casino after the first flights of TLCs disembarked the supporting engineers and tanks.

Labels on image: ANTI-TANK GUN, CASINO, WEST HEADLAND, CHÂTEAU, RUE DE SYGOGNE

Reconnaissance photograph taken by a Spitfire of No. 1 PRU Squadron, RAF, on August 21. German defences on and in the caves of the west headland included 75mm beach defence guns, 47mm and 37mm anti-tank guns, 80mm heavy mortars and numerous machine guns.

Note the left wing of the Casino partly destroyed. The Germans began demolishing it before the raid and completed it soon after. The casemate at the north-west corner, and the one in front at the north-east corner, sited 47mm and 37mm anti-tank guns respectively.

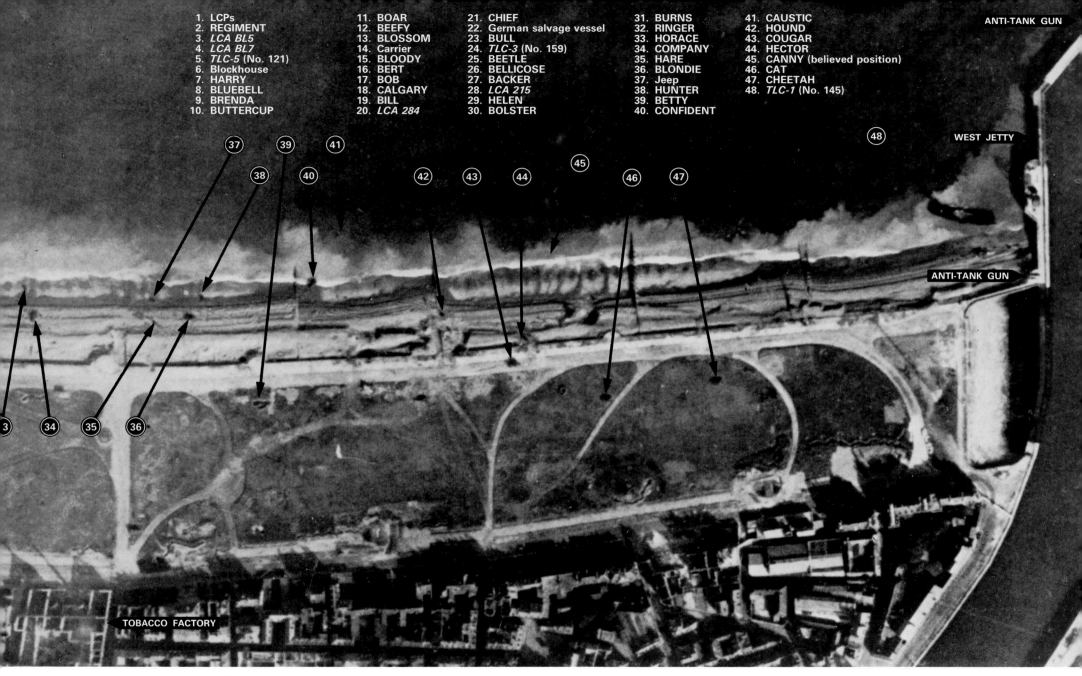

1. LCPs
2. REGIMENT
3. *LCA BL5*
4. *LCA BL7*
5. *TLC-5* (No. 121)
6. Blockhouse
7. HARRY
8. BLUEBELL
9. BRENDA
10. BUTTERCUP
11. BOAR
12. BEEFY
13. BLOSSOM
14. Carrier
15. BLOODY
16. BERT
17. BOB
18. CALGARY
19. BILL
20. *LCA 284*
21. CHIEF
22. German salvage vessel
23. BULL
24. *TLC-3* (No. 159)
25. BEETLE
26. BELLICOSE
27. BACKER
28. *LCA 215*
29. HELEN
30. BOLSTER
31. BURNS
32. RINGER
33. HORACE
34. COMPANY
35. HARE
36. BLONDIE
37. Jeep
38. HUNTER
39. BETTY
40. CONFIDENT
41. CAUSTIC
42. HOUND
43. COUGAR
44. HECTOR
45. CANNY (believed position)
46. CAT
47. CHEETAH
48. *TLC-1* (No. 145)

ANTI-TANK GUN

WEST JETTY

ANTI-TANK GUN

TOBACCO FACTORY

A 37mm gun was also located on the West Jetty. These caused heavy casualties among the assaulting forces. The many zig-zag trenches at the rear of the promenade sheltered many light machine gun posts. All the side streets were blocked by concrete anti-tank barriers, some with anti-tank guns mounted behind. However, the Rue de Sygogne did have an opening, with only a metal gate, to allow German vehicles access to the promenade. The tanks were to have advanced into the town using this street.

ALLOCATION OF 14th CANADIAN ARMY TANK REGIMENT TROOPS TO TANK LANDING CRAFT (TLC) FOR DIEPPE RAID

Flight	TLC	SubUnit	Key No.	Vehicle Name	W/D No.	Vehicle Type	Turret Number	Commander	Driver	Co-Driver	Gunner	Loader/Radio Operator
1	TLC-1	C Sqn HQ	[21]	CHIEF‡	T-31124R	CHURCHILL I	F1 in Circle	Maj A. Glenn (OC C Sqn)	Tpr L. A. Powers	Tpr F. R. Morton	Tpr L. A. Peridue	Cpl C. J. Vermilyea
	No. 145	F Troop	[34]	COMPANY	T-31878R	CHURCHILL I	F3 in Circle	Capt G. T. Valentine (2IC C Sqn)	Tpr O. G. Richards	Tpr J. W. Hilsabeck	Tpr J. C. Kind	Cpl W. W. Leach
			[18]	CALGARY*	T-68559	CHURCHILL III	F2 in Circle	Lt B. G. Douglas	Cpl J. H. P. McCann	Sgt A. S. Wagstaff	Tpr K. Smethurst	Tpr D. G. Scott
		HQ Sqn	[33]	HORACE	F-64318	Daimler S/C MkII	8 in Diamond		Tpr J. G. Hocken			Tpr V. F. Olliffe†
1	TLC-2	13 Troop	[43]	COUGAR‡	T-68173	CHURCHILL III	13 in Circle	Lt T. R. Cornett	Tpr G. R. Armstrong	Tpr R. H. Hill	Tpr G. M. Ross	Tpr A. R. Leithead
	No. 127		[47]	CHEETAH	T-62171	CHURCHILL III	13 in Circle	Cpl G. H. Wiggins	Tpr F. Hilsabeck	Tpr E. E. Farr	Tpr D. M. Jenkins	Tpr D. W. Scratch
			[46]	CAT*	T-68696	CHURCHILL III	13 in Circle	Sgt J. Weaver	Tpr N. F. Choveaux	Tpr J. R. Sommerville	Tpr W. L. McLellan	Tpr G. L. Blair
		HQ Sqn	[44]	HECTOR	F-64306	Daimler S/C MkII	9 in Diamond		Tpr A. E. Buckley			Tpr E. G. Anderson
1	TLC-3	8 Troop	[23]	BULL	T-31862	CHURCHILL I OKE	8 in Square	Capt D. G. Purdy†	Cpl W. D. Ibister	Tpr W. Stewart†	Tpr L. Hudson	Tpr P. W. Aide§
	No. 159		[11]	BOAR	T-32049	CHURCHILL I OKE	8 in Square	Sgt J. Sullivan	LCpl A. A. Poirier	Tpr A. R. Birston	Tpr E. Paquette	Tpr A. L. Chick
			[25]	BEETLE	T-68875	CHURCHILL I OKE	8 in Square	Lt G. L. Drysdale	Tpr R. F. Milne	Tpr R. F. Anderson	Tpr S. G. Hodgson	Tpr B. M. Skinner
				Bulldozer D7¶								
1A	TLC-4	B Sqn HQ	[31]	BURNS	T-31135R	CHURCHILL I	F1 in Square	Maj C. E. Page (OC B Sqn)	Cpl G. M. Mowat	Tpr T. G. Gorman†	Tpr W. E. Scheuchner	Tpr J. M. Dickie
	No. 126	F Troop	[27]	BACKER	T-68352	CHURCHILL II	F2 in Square	Lt R. H. Wallace	Tpr E. M. Snider	Tpr J. A. Chapman	Tpr C. L. Provis†	Cpl J. O. Cote
			[30]	BOLSTER*	T-31107R	CHURCHILL I	F3 in Square	Sgt T. R. Cunningham	Tpr J. A. Booker	Tpr G. E. Hailes	Cpl E. S. Porter	Tpr S. A. Bell
		HQ Sqn	[29]	HELEN		Daimler S/C MkII	6 in Diamond		Tpr A. K. Thompson			Tpr W. D. P. Sawers
1A	TLC-5	9 Troop	[10]	BUTTERCUP‡	T-31655	CHURCHILL III	9 in Square	Sgt J. D. Morrison	Tpr L. H. Johnstone	Tpr J. G. Walker	Tpr A. Heffer	Tpr S. H. Edwards
	No. 121		[13]	BLOSSOM	T-68561R	CHURCHILL III	9 in Square	Lt M. J. A. Lambert	Tpr L. G. Twa	Cpl W. H. Wigley	Tpr H. A. Embree	Tpr J. L. Whitely
			[8]	BLUEBELL*	T-68759R	CHURCHILL III	9 in Square	Cpl D. L. Brownlee	Tpr M. Holden	Tpr G. Volk§	Tpr A. R. Watson	Tpr W. C. McBryan
		HQ Sqn	[7]	HARRY		Daimler S/C MkII	7 in Diamond		Cpl A. A. Butler			Tpr A. E. Graham
1A	TLC-6	6 Troop	[17]	BOB	T-68557R	CHURCHILL III	6 in Square	Lt J. H. Dunlap	Tpr J. H. Cox	Tpr A. L. Johnson	Cpl T. Bereton	Tpr H. J. Ganshirt
	No. 163		[16]	BERT	T-68560R	CHURCHILL III	6 in Square	SSM G. M. Menzies	Tpr N. A. McArthur	Tpr T. A. Dunsmore	Tpr W. G. Stewart	Tpr F. H. Noel
			[19]	BILL	T-68558R	CHURCHILL III	6 in Square	Cpl C. A. Heck	Tpr E. E. Schlapkohl	Tpr J. D. White	Tpr J. O. Hunter	Tpr L. A. Herzog
				Bulldozer D7¶								
2	TLC-7	10 Troop	[12]	BEEFY	T-68177R	CHURCHILL III	10 in Square	Sgt H. R. Patrick	Tpr M. A. McIntyre	Tpr R. A. Lincoln	Cpl W. J. Hunt	Tpr R. A. Gilbert
	No. 124		[26]	BELLICOSE	T-68175	CHURCHILL III	10 in Square	Lt E. Bennett	Tpr R. C. Cornelssen†	Tpr L. Storvold	Tpr W. E. Stannard	Tpr A. F. Anderson
			[15]	BLOODY*	T-68701R	CHURCHILL III	10 in Square	Sgt R. B. Lee	Tpr C. V. Richardson	Tpr A. W. Hill	Tpr D. R. Lazier	Tpr C. M. Staples
		HQ Sqn	[38]	HUNTER		Daimler S/C MkII	1 in Diamond		Tpr M. F. Zima†			Maj G. M. Rolfe (RCCS)
				Jeep¶								
2	TLC-8	Regtl.HQ	[32]	RINGER	T-68881	CHURCHILL II	Z2 in Diamond	Capt A. G. Stanton (Adj.)	Cpl F. Makaroff	Tpr J. J. Mayhew	Tpr F. A. Tanner	Tpr T. H. Pinder
	No. 125		[2]	REGIMENT	T-31923R	CHURCHILL II	Z1 in Diamond	Lt-Col J. G. Andrews (CO)†	LCpl G. A. Nelson	Cpl T. L. Carnie	Tpr P. Friesen†	Sgt C. Rienhart
				ROUNDER¶	T-68452	CHURCHILL II	Z3 in Diamond	Maj John Begg (2IC)				
				Universal Carrier¶								
				Jeep¶								
2	TLC-9	7 Troop	[9]	BRENDA	T-68760R	CHURCHILL III	7 in Square	Sgt W. W. Olive	Tpr J. W. Horne	Tpr R. H. Clark	Tpr B. H. Clifton	Tpr E. Taylor
	No. 166		[39]	BETTY	T-68176R	CHURCHILL III	7 in Square	Lt A. L. Breithaupt	Cpl J. K. Nash	Tpr J. P. Halase	Tpr M. Leithead	Tpr H. A. Stanfield
			[36]	BLONDIE*	T-68880	CHURCHILL III	7 in Square	Cpl D. W. G. Jordon	Tpr E. Dannewald	Tpr D. H. McCaskill	Tpr L. N. Harned	Tpr P. Armstrong
		HQ Sqn	[35]	HARE	F-64319	Daimler S/C MkII	3 in Diamond		Tpr K. Doda			Cpl Chambers (RCCS)
			[37]	Jeep	CM4218884		Z3 on bumper		Tpr E. Huscroft†			
2	TLC-10	15 Troop	[41]	CAUSTIC	T-68702	CHURCHILL III	15 in Circle	Lt A. B. Patterson	Cpl D. F. Craigie	Tpr C. M. Hooey	Tpr C. J. Anderson	Tpr J. A. Nyman
	No. 165		[45]	CANNY	T-68870	CHURCHILL III	15 in Circle	Sgt N. R. Thompson	Tpr C. S. Brawner	Tpr G. A. McNicol	Tpr E. Twemlow	Tpr T. K. Reilly
			[40]	CONFIDENT*	T-68704R	CHURCHILL III	15 in Circle	Cpl R. W. Dowling	Tpr L. Patterson	Tpr R. H. Johnston	Tpr J. J. Pewtress	Tpr S. B. Playdon
		HQ Sqn	[42]	HOUND	F-64306	Daimler S/C MkII	2 in Diamond		LCpl F. Howe§			LCpl A. G. Wills (RCCS)
				Jeep¶								

* These seven tanks each towed ashore a Daimler Scout Car with a driver and one radio operator (14 CATR) or (RCCS).

‡ These three leading tanks carried the track-laying device. The track-laying equipment for the other lead tanks, BOB and BURNS, had been damaged in transit and had been removed before landing. The lead tank in *TLC-3*, BULL, could not be fitted with the track-laying equipment because of its flame-thrower apparatus.

† Killed in action (plus SSM A. H. Tough and Cpl D. E. Welch of White Beach Party).   ¶ Did not land.   § Landed but returned to UK.

The Calgary Tanks Arrive
HEADQUARTERS FIGHTING (F) TROOP, C SQUADRON

Flight 1 consisted of three TLCs which landed between approximately 0525 and 0530 hours (five to ten minutes late). *TLC-1* (No. 145) [48 on plan on pages 10–11 and 64] touched down on the eastern end of Red Beach holding C Squadron Headquarters F Troop, consisting of the tanks CHIEF [21], COMPANY [34] and CALGARY [18], as well as the scout car HORACE [33]. On landing, the TLC received several direct hits from shore batteries. After disembarking all vehicles, continuous hits partially sank and stranded it in shallow water.

CHIEF [21], commanded by Major Allen Glenn, Officer Commanding C Squadron, was the first tank out and prematurely used the chespaling track-laying device to advance to the high ridge of stones before jettisoning the whole apparatus. On the other side, however, was a wide trench about seven feet deep running the entire length of the beach to the Casino. Tidal action on the chert had created this trench and German excavations of rubble for the building of fortifications had deepened it. From the ridge, however, Major Glenn had a good view, when not obscured by smoke, of the promenade and both flanks of the beach and therefore kept his tank on the beach. Many years later he wrote that 'this was a logical place to set up a command post to observe all action and give support' and that 'it was only close to the end of the action that CHIEF was moved west, along the ridge to observe other developments'. After moving down the beach to the area in front of the Casino, CHIEF then returned the way it had come. On arriving at the beached *TLC-3*, CHIEF stopped at the western end of it, broadside, to provide more protection for the men sheltering behind the TLC. Inset shows a German sailor triumphantly removing the command pennant.

COMPANY [34], commanded by Captain George T. Valentine, landed and was about to turn right after CHIEF when a shell hit the left front drive wheel, breaking a track pin and immobilising the tank just in front of the ridge on the beach. The co-driver, Trooper James W. Hilsabeck, recalls that after clearing the water proofing around his 3-inch howitzer with a smoke shell, he did not have enough elevation to shoot over the ridge which the infantry was using for cover. The crew could only use the 2-pounder and Besa machine gun in the turret. The tank was hit by mortar shells several times and although it filled with smoke there were no injuries by the time of surrender.

CALGARY [18], the last out, was under the command of C Squadron's recently appointed reconnaissance officer, Lieutenant Brice G. Douglas. Towing HORACE [33], it turned right, proceeding parallel to the sea-wall towards the Casino, looking for a place to cross onto the promenade. About halfway down White Beach its left track was suddenly blown. Although HORACE, carrying Trooper John G. Hocken and Trooper Victor F. Olliffe, released within fifteen feet of landing, it immediately received a shot through the right side of its turret. Probably due to the explosives or ammunition it carried, it caught fire and Trooper Olliffe was killed. In the picture *opposite*, the hulk of COMPANY can be seen in the background on the right. CALGARY spent the rest of the day acting as a pillbox, concentrating its 6-pounder fire on predetermined targets such as the Casino, initially, and the tobacco factory. The loader-operator of CALGARY, Trooper Dennis G. Scott, describes this action: 'We were sitting with no cover and so had a good view of the beach. Lieutenant Douglas found enough targets to keep [his gunner Trooper Ken] Smethurst busy until we had used up all our ammunition. Once we observed horses pulling mortars or guns along the top of the [west] cliff to the Château, Smethurst hesitated because he really did not want to shoot the horses. Meanwhile we were attracting a lot of gun-fire. We took some direct hits on the turret, hard enough that the paint was melting and running down on the inside. The heat inside, along with the smell of the smoke and cordite, was almost unbearable, so much so that Sergeant Alfred S. Wagstaff, who was down in the co-driver's seat, was put out of action. We stayed in the tank until we were ordered to surrender.'

13 TROOP, C SQUADRON

TLC-2 (No. 127) touched down near the West Jetty at the east end of the beach. It soon became a focal point for German coastal artillery, anti-aircraft guns, machine guns and mortars. 13 Troop of C Squadron, under Troop Leader Lieutenant Thomas R. Cornett, quickly left the TLC after the engineers moved some of their wounded clear. Cornett's tank, COUGAR [43], successfully crossed the beach and the sea-wall, using its chespaling, jettisoned part of its apparatus and turned right. On crossing over the wall, COUGAR turned right and was immediately fired upon by a well-sited 75-mm coastal gun, positioned on the far side of the canal below the east headland. A shell hit the turret ring and jammed it. CAT [46] aimed its 6-pounder at this enemy position and silenced it. COUGAR, after concentrating its 6-pounder fire on the tobacco factory, broke its left track while manoeuvring, because chert rocks lodged between the bogey wheel and treads. The tank briefly manoeuvred with one track before it too was blown by shell-fire. The crew evacuated and went back to the beach looking for cover. Trooper Gerald M. Ross, the gunner, stayed behind to burn out the interior of the tank with a sticky bomb.

The next tank, CHEETAH [47], attempted to follow the lead tank over the wall but had problems in climbing onto the promenade. Its driver, Trooper Fred Hilsabeck (brother of James, the co-driver of COMPANY) recalled that he tried to drive as straight as possible, so as to avoid getting the rocks built up behind the bogey wheels. The first time CHEETAH tried to climb the wall, the tank's exposed belly was hit by a shell which, he vividly describes: 'Turned red hot right at my feet, so it came mighty close to coming through . . . It blew all the fuses in the tank, so we rolled back down in behind the wall. I got all the fuses changed with a flashlight, got it started up again and then we went up over the wall . . . Once we were

upon the promenade we were like a bunch of rats in a treadmill. We didn't know where to go or just what to do.' TLC-2 also had Major Sucharov and his Beach Assault Party of 15 men aboard. Since all of 13 Troop's tanks had successfully made it on to the esplanade, they were no longer needed in this area. Major Sucharov decided that landing at the east end of the beach would mean carrying all timber and materials to the right on foot. 'Under existing fire the loss in men would have been too heavy.' He asked the captain to put in more to the west but additional shell fire so damaged the craft, it had to withdraw. Thus, none of the assault engineers or the mortar detachment landed.

CAT, the last tank out, towed HECTOR [44] across the beach and over the sea-wall, although HECTOR's driver, Trooper Edward G. Anderson, and radio operator, Trooper Art E. Buckley, recall that they drove up onto the esplanade under their own power. HECTOR was the only scout car to cross over the wall and it drove around unable to penetrate the town before returning to the waterfront. A mortar bomb explosion flipped it 360 degrees and threw its occupants out. They took immediate cover by the wall. CAT and CHEETAH cruised up and down the esplanade for hours, firing their machine guns at the German positions in the sea-front buildings and trenches, and using the 6-pounders on German strong points, the Casino and headlands. Ju 87 'Stuka' dive-bombers attacking the tanks throughout the battle, finally hit the engine in the back of CAT and the flash of the bomb went up underneath the skirt of the turret. The loader-operator, Trooper George L. Blair, was temporarily blinded, and the gunner, Trooper W. Lloyd McLellan, was burned and wounded. Since the escape doors were sealed by the waterproofing, Sergeant Jack Weaver, the crew commander, quickly climbed

out the turret and pulled off the waterproofing to allow the crew to escape. CHEETAH came by to give cover and to evacuate the two wounded to the beach. Sergeant Weaver then spread some sticky bombs in CAT and set them off, took some grenades and a machine gun, and ran towards the beach, being forced to take cover, periodically, by machine gun and mortar fire. Meanwhile, CHEETAH was heading towards the beach when the same Stuka came in for another pass. Trooper Hilsabeck still remembers the bomb coming straight for his periscope, then levelling off at the last minute, and finally hitting the engine compartment. The hydraulic system was hit, and he recalls that 'the motor went wild, there was no clutch or steering and the radio was out'. Corporal George H. Wiggins, the crew commander, ordered him to shut off the engine and the crew to get out through the left side escape hatch. The crew of CHEETAH and the two wounded troopers from CAT remained on the sheltered side of the tank until the surrender. Snipers consistently harassed them from the West Jetty area and finally wounded Fred Hilsabeck.

TLC-3 (No. 159) [24] carried the naval and tank beach parties. Captain Allan H. Turney, HQ Squadron second-in-command (2IC), was the Senior Assistant Military Landing Officer (Tank) [SAMLO(T)] White Beach, and was assisted by Squadron Sergeant-Major Alexander H. Tough and Corporal Dwight E. Welch of B Squadron. Captain Cyril R. Eldred, HQ Squadron Technical Officer, was the AMLO(T) Red Beach, and was assisted by C Squadron Sergeant-Major Robert Cordner and Corporal Vern C. Leonard. (Sergeant-Major Tough and Corporal Welch were later killed.) Their duties included guiding the reserve flights to their objectives, directing medical and ammunition parties on the beaches and liaising with the beach headquarters of the Principal Beach Master (PBM), Commander G. T. Lambert, Royal Navy, and his opposite number, the Principal Military Landing Officer (PMLO), Major Brian S. McCool, of the Royal Regiment of Canada. Corporal Leonard recalls that for recognition purposes, each tank beach party had their helmets painted blue, red or yellow, corresponding to their squadron colour, and had similarly-coloured 3in×4in flags to mark the streets along which the tanks would withdraw to their beach rendezvous points. *TLC-3* also carried a bulldozer and tanks of 8 Troop B Squadron, under Troop Leader Captain Douglas G. 'Spike' Purdy, equipped with the Oke flame-thrower.

At approximately 0525 hours, about one hundred yards from the junction of Red and White Beaches, a naval rating lowered the ramp half way to give Captain Purdy, in his tank BULL [23], a preview of the shore. Believing the TLC had reached the beach, Captain Purdy ordered his driver to go forward. They could not hear the warning shouts from men nearby since the tank was closed down. The tank moved forward and the ramp collapsed. BULL sank in about ten feet of water *(left)* and the crew abandoned it. Trooper Percy W. Aide, the loader-operator, recalls what happened: 'When we went out, I remember Captain Purdy saying "We are running behind time . . . " All I could hear, when I got the order to switch on the [wireless] set, was nothing but guttural German commands, excited commands, crackling all over the place. Then I heard Captain Purdy say, "driver advance", and we just rolled ahead a few feet and the left front side of the ramp went down and hesitated a second. The lights in the tank went out and the engine went off. Corporal Isbister, the driver, kicked it in again, the lights came back on, the motor started and then drowned. Then there was that pause in between where it seemed to me that a couple in the [ramp] chain had sprung and she [BULL] nosed right down. That's when the water started to pour in all over the place, from a thousand different sources . . . The boat was in reverse then, struggling to get back and it was whipping from right to left, trying to shake the tank off. It had to back up into deep water to get it off, and as it did that I pushed [the turret hatch] just as they shook one way and the thing flew open. They never did get the other door open because everyone poured out of the one aperture on the left side.' Captain Purdy could not swim and, although Trooper Aide tried to save him, he drowned, his body later being washed up on shore. The co-driver, Trooper W. 'Pipe Smoking Bill' Stewart was last seen swimming out to sea, while the other two members of the crew made it to shore. Trooper Aide was wounded and was evacuated, one of the only two tank crewmen to have landed and returned to England. As *TLC-3* came in again, a shell obliterated the wheel house and killed all its personnel. The TLC ended up grounded in the shallow water at an angle pointing east, about thirty yards west of the tobacco factory, and was so badly damaged it was unable to move. *Above:* The interior of *TLC-3* — the sheet-steel air intake from BULL can be seen on the left with the front of a D7 bulldozer behind. Note the hydrogen gas cylinders for a barrage balloon.

Ten minutes after BULL's unfortunate exit, the second tank, BOAR [11], in making a heavy landing from the rampless TLC, knocked off its flame thrower fuel tank. The driver, Lance-Corporal Arthur A. 'Ack Ack' Poirier, who had previous catskinning experience as a farmer, could feel when rocks were starting to build up behind the track wheels and knew he had to drive straight for a time to clear them out. BOAR proceeded west down the beach and crossed onto the promenade in the area of the Casino. It remained mobile throughout the morning before being ordered back to the beach to cover the withdrawal. At that time the crew was ordered to immobilise the tank and use it as a fort. This is the best picture available showing the front of BOAR on the right with the flame-thrower. BUTTERCUP and BLUEBELL lie behind with *TLC-5* in the background.

The third tank, BEETLE [25], under the command of Lieutenant Gordon L. Drysdale, started up but could not move forward. The tank reversed, crushing two wounded soldiers in its path. Unfortunately, the left track chock had not been removed, the men responsible probably having become casualties. BEETLE landed heavily, blew its lighting system and had to operate with its emergency supply. After turning left, Lieutenant Drysdale soon heard a general announcement from Lieutenant Edwin Bennett, 10 Troop, B Squadron, that he could cross over the sea-wall in the area of the Casino. As Lieutenant Drysdale turned, a pin in BEETLE's right track broke because of the build-up of rocks. For the remainder of the day, BEETLE remained immobilised at the eastern end of Red Beach, acting as a pillbox.

Lieutenant Drysdale ordered his crew to watch for muzzle flashes from the west headland, and his gunner, Trooper Sydney G. Hodgson, fired back at them. Later, Lieutenant Drysdale left the tank to check the damaged track, but realising it was unfixable, kept his crew in the tank. The tank also protected others who had gathered behind it, including Major Charles E. Page, Officer Commanding B Squadron, and Sergeant Tommy R. Cunningham, also of B Squadron Headquarters F Troop. Lieutenant Drysdale, taking his tank's Bren gun, took cover behind the right side of the disabled tank and started firing on the west headland. His firing brought a heavy response from machine guns and mortars. Automatic fire hitting the water below him was so intense it reminded him of rain.

Left: **Flight 1A landed a few minutes after the first flight on White Beach. *TLC-4* (No. 126) came in just east of the tobacco factory carrying Major Page, and B Squadron Headquarters F Troop consisting of tanks BURNS [31], BACKER [27], and BOLSTER [30] and scout car HELEN [29]. After landing all the vehicles, the TLC withdew while receiving constant shellfire. The Senior Flotilla Officer, TLCs, Red and White Beaches, Lieutenant-Commander Cyril M. Masterman (RANVR), later reported that it was 'sinking by the stern with the engine room and mess decks flooded'. He ordered LCP(L)s alongside to evacuate it.**

Above: **Disembarking in under three minutes, Major Page, in BURNS, headed across the beach over the first wire to the crest of the ridge: 'I gave orders to turn to the right and that's when I was hit . . . the right track was blown off. The left one went on for a few seconds and kind of pulled me into the trench.' Since the tank was immobilised pointing downward into the ditch and thus unable to use its weapons, he ordered the crew to bail out and take whatever cover they could beside the sea-wall. Corporal Gordon M. Mowat, the driver, was wounded and Trooper Thomas G. Gorman, the co-driver, was killed later in the morning.**

Just as the second tank, BACKER [27], left the TLC, it received a direct hit *(right)* on the turret ring which prevented the turret from traversing. BACKER's commander, Lieutenant R. H. 'Dick' Wallace, followed the path of BURNS, went around it turning westwards, advanced about another hundred yards before being immobilised either by a direct hit on the left track or more likely by the stones breaking the left track. Lieutenant Wallace had intended handing the tank over to Major Page, in accordance with operating procedure. The tank was now almost parallel to the sea-wall pointing west. The 2-pounder in the immobilised turret was pointing straight ahead down the beach and was therefore ineffective. In order to get its main armament and second Besa machine gun into action, the co-driver, Trooper Jack A. Chapman, crawled out the left side escape hatch to attach a strong cable to the gun turret. As the driver, Trooper Earl M. Snider, reversed the track, it pulled the gun around so they could fire on the houses west of the Casino. After firing off all ammunition, the crew blew up the interior of the tank and took cover. Trooper Chapman recalls BACKER's gunner, Trooper Charles 'Heavy' Provis: 'He was killed teaching me. He was an old infantry man with the Seaforth Highlanders, a hell of a guy, there was never a better guy on earth. Of course, I had never had any association with infantry and once we abandoned the tank, he taught me how to crawl along on your belly from where our tank was to the beach . . . I was right beside "Heavy," that's what we called him, "Heavy" Provis. He was a big guy and that's the reason he got shot. He couldn't get in the hole we were in totally and his head was sticking out . . . when he got shot right between the eyes.' Lieutenant Wallace *(inset right)* recalled that 'After the surrender I spent the rest of the day on the beach looking after the wounded. I am very sure I was the last Canadian officer to leave the beach (under escort) about 9.30 p.m.'

The third tank BOLSTER [30] successfully towed off HELEN, carrying Troopers William D. P. Sawers and Albert K. Thompson but, before they could detach the tow cable linked to the Churchill, the Daimler scout car immediately bellied in the chert directly behind the tank. Photographs of BOLSTER and HELEN show the tow cable still attached. The burned-out interior of the scout car was probably the result of hits on the stores by tracer fire or sabotage by the crew on evacuation. BOLSTER was still climbing the beach when its right track was broken by the build up of chert rocks and it came to a full stop in the area of the beached *TLC-3*. Although the tank could not move, it continued firing its 2-pounder and 3-inch howitzer until it ran out of ammunition. Its gunner, Corporal Elmer S. Porter, recalls silencing an anti-tank gun in the west cliff before evacuating. (We previously saw BOLSTER on page 3.)

TLC-5 (No. 121) [5] touched down in front of the Casino and unloaded its tanks but very accurate mortar and artillery fire wiped out the crew, leaving the blazing craft beached in front of the Casino. (We saw her during training on page 4.) The craft carried the tanks of 9 Troop, B Squadron, under Troop Leader Lieutenant Marcel J. A. Lambert.

All tanks and scout car HARRY [7] landed dry; BUTTERCUP [10], under the command of Troop Sergeant John D. 'JD' Morrison, leading the way and laying down the chespaling tracks. Sergeant Morrison recalls that to activate the track-laying device and simultaneously blow off the waterproofing and louvre extensions, he just had to hold the plug about an inch from the socket and the sparks would set it off. Unfortunately, it also shorted out the 'B' (inter-troop communication) set of his radio, and the only way that Lieutenant Lambert could contact BUTTERCUP was through the regimental 'A' net. Sergeant Morrison also remembers how on advancing up the beach, enemy shell-fire was hitting his 6-pounder gun mantelet, causing the paint to peel on the inside of the tank. It successfully crossed the beach, wire and sea-wall and, then, for the remainder of the action, concentrated its fire on the west headland and on the seafront buildings behind and to the west of the Casino. Later it returned to the beach below the Casino that gave some cover from the intense fire coming from the west headland. The driver, Trooper Lloyd H. Johnstone, positioned the tank parallel to the water's edge to allow the crew some protection on evacuation. The crew could not blow up the interior of the tank because too many wounded infantry instantly sheltered beside it.

The second tank, BLOSSOM [13], under Lieutenant Lambert, attempted to follow the path of the first tank using the laid chespaling tracks but swerved off the chespaling, breaking its right track in the rocks and stopping sideways across the chespaling. Lieutenant Lambert remembers the situation well: 'We were doing a turn to get lined up with the wall, where Sergeant Morrison had gone over, when our right track broke . . . we had never run into that kind of stuff before . . . once we had broken our track we were pretty much sheltered by the Casino [in the left background of the picture] and, therefore, the mortar and artillery shells that came lobbing over, because of their trajectory, landed behind us in the water . . . A couple of times things popped in, on one occasion, something hit me on my hat badge,

either a bit of rock or shrapnel, and then fell down my gunner's [Trooper Henry A. 'Al' Embree] neck, it was hot because Embree reacted quite vigorously!' Remaining stationary for the rest of the morning, BLOSSOM directed its fire at targets on the west headland and a 37-mm gun in a blockhouse [6] situated at the north-east corner of the Casino. Lieutenant Lambert describes this blockhouse as being so well built with concrete of superior quality that the 6-pounder's armour-piercing shells had little effect; 'it was just like chipping away with a hand-pick . . . or spitting at it, we were terribly undergunned.' Luckily, for the crew of BLOSSOM, the tank had become immobilised at an angle to the east side of the blockhouse and, therefore, was not exposed to its field of fire.

The third tank, BLUEBELL [8], towing HARRY [7], attempted to go around BLOSSOM but became bogged down in the loose chert, immediately in front of the Casino, only able to move back and forth a few feet, while firing its weapons. The co-driver of BLUEBELL, Trooper George Volk, describes how the crew, through the tank's telescopic sight, finally picked up the flash of the barrel of an annoying German sniper situated on the Casino roof.

A round from the 6-pounder demolished the area. Later, Trooper Volk was ordered out of the tank to unhitch HARRY they were towing and to see if he could clear the rocks away from the tracks. In doing so, he was wounded and eventually evacuated as a casualty, the only tank crew member, besides Trooper Percy Aide of BULL, to have landed and subsequently returned to England.

HARRY [7], driven by Corporal Arnold A. Butler with Trooper Andrew E. Graham as the radio operator, bogged down part way up the beach. For about an hour, BLUEBELL and HARRY attempted to negotiate the loose chert but the manoeuvres, and spinning the wheels, only served to dig HARRY deeper into the rocks. Corporal Butler recalls that 'Where we were, there was no way you could move with the scout car . . . It was too steep to go up in the gravel and rocks . . . We knew that once we unhooked we couldn't get up.' All the scout cars were towed ashore with a single steel cable connecting their right front bumper to a hitch on the rear of the tank, with a pin to pull out once the car crossed the sea-wall. Corporal Butler explains that 'We had a wire up over so we could pull that pin out. Well the pin with a heavy jerk wouldn't come out. We had to get out and pound it out with a rock . . . with the help of [Trooper Volk and] a couple of infantry who were hiding behind our armoured car. Once you had pounded it out, we couldn't go anywhere except backwards.'

6 TROOP, B SQUADRON

TLC-6 (No. 163) attempted three times to come in but had three helmsmen killed. On its fourth attempt, it used the sinking *TLC-1* as cover and was able to land the tanks dry. Probably due to the intense fire, the Calgary Highlanders of Canada 3-inch mortar detachment of 21 men, and the D7 bulldozer, were unable to disembark. The TLC passed a rope to *TLC-1* in an attempt to tow her off but the line was shot away. *TLC-6* was forced to leave her. Lieutenant Jack H. Dunlap in BOB [17] was Troop Leader of 6 Troop, B Squadron, and recalls that 'We were out in the Channel behind a smoke-screen, about one mile off the beach, when we were informed that we would be going in. I ordered the crews into their tank positions, the motors were started with no trouble and radio communications were

tested. We came out of the smoke-screen into brilliant sunshine and, before closing my hatch, I had one last look at the beach over the top of the ramp. It appeared to be not far away and a look to the rear of the landing craft showed the two tanks closed down . . . We rammed into the beach, the ramp went down and I moved my tank BOB down the ramp and to the right along the water's edge. We fired the charges under the waterproofing as we moved towards the Casino. However, when we test fired the Besa machine guns, the turret Besa jammed from a double feed. We stopped just long enough to clear the jammed Besa, called BERT and BILL, and the three tanks took off up the beach, over the sea-wall by the Casino and drove out on the promenade.'

BERT [16] was the second tank off, turned left and halted. At this time, the gunner of BERT, Trooper William G. Stewart, realised that the turret was not traversing because of the inadequate blowing of the waterproofing. The co-driver, Trooper Thomas A. Dunsmore, went out and cut the turret loose with a machete. Later in the morning, while manoeuvring in the area immediately to the east of the Casino, BERT had its left track blown off. Its crew would have been killed instantly if they had attempted to fix the track so they stayed inside. In this picture, the camouflaged Casino can be seen on the right with the Château on the west headland behind.

They were in a position, though, to give covering fire to about 20 men of the Royal Hamilton Light Infantry who crossed from the Casino into the town. Lieutenant Dunlap explains that: 'I ordered Corporal Heck, in BILL, to go alongside and take off three of BERT's crew. It took some time because they had to cut through the waterproofing covering the side hatches, with the tank's machete. When they had the three crewmen, my tank BOB moved alongside and took the remaining two crew members, one of whom was Sergeant Menzies.' Here, German engineers use BERT to tow CHIEF onto the promenade. Note the tobacco factory behind which COHQ planners wrongly identified as an ammunition dump.

BILL [19], the last tank, disembarked without problem and followed BERT onto the promenade. The troop then headed towards the rear of the Casino, firing at strong points in the area of the Château on the west headland. As Lieutenant Dunlap remembers: 'Just as we got behind the Casino, we received a radio call from Lieutenant Marcel Lambert, 9 Troop, B Squadron, that a 37-mm gun was firing from a concrete bunker [6] on the east end of the Casino. I moved BOB into position and we fired into an opening at the rear of the bunker. We also fired the turret Besa but it again jammed, so we forgot about it for the rest of the day. I turned the bunker over to Sergeant Menzies, in BERT, and moved to fire the 6-pounder at a sandbagged gun emplacement at the side of a building facing the promenade. We destroyed

it. We spotted German infantry running across the promenade at the extreme east end, toward and into a slit trench, but we were unable to bring the bow Besa on target in time to do any damage. I could see no way off the street because of the concrete road blocks, so we moved about firing at suspected targets on the western headland.' The co-driver of BILL, Trooper John D. White, recalls that what was probably a sniper shot and smashed the thick glass of the driver's vision port forcing the driver, Trooper Elmer Schlapkohl, to rely on the extremely limited vision through his periscope. Eventually BOB and BILL returned to the beach to lay down a smoke-screen to cover the withdrawal but Lieutenant Dunlap realised that his men had little chance of evacuation.

At about 0605 hours, Flight 2 of four TLCs landed on schedule, drawing extremely heavy fire. *TLC-7* (No. 124), carrying 10 Troop of B Squadron, under Troop Leader Lieutenant Edwin 'Ed' Bennett, landed in the centre of Red and White Beaches. On the way in, the gun emplacement on the jetty put a shell through the side of the TLC. It ricocheted off a tank turret and hit the barrage balloon storage area, exploding some hydrogen cylinders and setting the balloons on fire. The flaming rubberised material settled on the rear of the troop commander's tank BELLICOSE [26]. A piece of metal from the explosion hit Lieutenant Bennett's right eye while the flames burned off all his hair. He ordered the crew to put out the fire. His radio operator, Trooper Archie F. Anderson, got out of the tank and used a nearby fire extinguisher to good effect. (Anderson was awarded the Military Medal for this and other brave acts he carried out during and after the battle.) The explosion also jammed the turret so it could not rotate. BEEFY [12] was the first tank out, landing dry, and immediately blew the waterproofing, but to remove fabric still around the turret ring the co-driver, Trooper Roy A. 'Abe' Lincoln, had to climb out on top of the moving tank which was under enemy small arms fire. BEEFY temporarily halted about thirty feet off the ramp to get its bearings. Lieutenant Bennett, although severely wounded, went in with BELLICOSE *(above)*. An ammunition party consisting of Lance-Corporal C. E. D. 'Chuck' Suffel, Trooper Franklin D. 'Tiny' Bevan and others, had tied a sled loaded with tank ammunition to the back of BELLICOSE. Unfortunately, it did not slide very well on the steel TLC and the tow cable snapped. Since they could do nothing about it they took what cover they could against the sea-wall and in bomb craters. Passing BEEFY, Lieutenant Bennett instructed his driver, Trooper R. C. 'Bobby' Cornelssen, to turn right towards the Casino. His reasons were sound: 'I had seen all the other tanks in the centre of the beach stranded in the shingle [chert]. We may have had a better chance on the beach because we didn't land as high up as the first flight of tanks. With the tide going out, it may not have been as loose shingle as it was higher up . . . I decided that we would stick to the water line and go along until we could see a place where we could go over the sea-wall.' Lieutenant Bennett found the chert piled up to within two feet of the wall near the Casino and crossed without problem. The rest of his troop followed. (After landing all its tanks and the scout car, *TLC-7* withdrew badly damaged and sank with a 14 CATR Jeep aboard.) On crossing onto the promenade, all three of Lieutenant Bennett's tanks went up the east side of the Casino towards the buildings fronting the promenade. On the way, his third tank, BLOODY, dropped into an anti-tank ditch. BEEFY gave covering fire while Troopers Donald R. Lazier and Austin W. 'Aussie' Hill attached a tow line, constantly under fire, and BEEFY pulled BLOODY out of the ditch. Sergeant Lee then dismounted to inspect the tank and he noticed that one of the left treads was partly cracked so BLOODY drove slowly and carefully while on the promenade.

Lieutenant Bennett, noticing some men of the Royal Hamilton Light Infantry pointing to something, turned his troop down the Boulevard de Verdun in front of the buildings. The troop proceeded down the full length of the boulevard, clearing the Germans out of slit trenches and giving the tanks' gunners easy targets, although BELLICOSE had to rotate the whole tank to compensate for the jammed turret. All the roads exiting the promenade were blocked with concrete barriers which were as high as eight feet and four feet thick with a firing step on the rear. At one point in the battle, the gunner of BEEFY, Corporal W. J. 'Billy' Hunt, spotted a sniper in a third storey window. Unable to get a proper sighting, he dropped the 6-pounder's breech block, lined up on the sniper through the barrel, then fired. Apparently he hit several snipers in this manner.

BLOODY [15] was the last tank out towing the scout car HUNTER [38]. This scout car, driven by Trooper Micheal F. Zima, carried Major Gordon M. 'Shorty' Rolfe, Royal Canadian Corps of Signals (RCCS), and his two No. 19 wireless sets. Rolfe commanded 1st Canadian Army Tank Brigade (1 CATB) Signals and was on loan to The Calgary Regiment for the operation on the specific request of the Regimental Commanding Officer, Lieutenant-Colonel Johnny G. Andrews. He had three scout cars under his command, HUNTER, HOUND and HARE, each with one 14 CATR driver and one signalman, and was supposed to report to Brigadier William W. Southam's 6th Infantry Brigade Headquarters at St Remy Church to co-ordinate the withdrawal between infantry and tanks. Sergeant Ron B. Lee, the crew commander of BLOODY, realising he could not cross the wall in this area, stopped, reversed and started crushing HUNTER and its occupants. Major Rolfe quickly pushed the warning button on the rear of the tank which stopped reversing and then moved right. Major Rolfe recalled: 'I guess the scout car looked like a derelict to the enemy but my radio sets were unharmed and operated all through the operation.'

'Scout cars HOUND [42] and HARE [35] were knocked out on landing from other TLCs', continues Major Rolfe. 'Lance-Corporal A. G. Wills (HOUND's RCCS radio operator), however, was not injured, made his way to HUNTER and became my operator until we surrendered along with the rest. Shortly after landing, I saw Brigadier Southam on the beach and made my way to him. He said his communications were completely non-existent because a tank had run over and destroyed the Signals "baby carriage". I told him we could cover any frequency he wanted and he was with me lying beside the scout car for most of the time. (The side opposite the west headland, of course.) About an hour after landing, my CAC driver, Michael Zima, received a mortar shell fragment which proved fatal. I rendered aid but it was ineffective.' Rolfe and his operator, by quickly switching frequencies, were able to maintain contact with the Headquarters' ship *Calpe* and the TLCs offshore, and the infantry and tank squadron commanders on shore. At one point, Trooper Len Storvold, the co-driver of BELLICOSE, found that his Besa machine gun jammed from overheating. He recollects that 'I poured oil over it to cool it down and damned near choked everyone from the smoke. It did get the gun working again.' BELLICOSE only returned to the beach to repair its steering system which had been damaged by frequent anti-tank hits. Once the damage had been fixed, BELLICOSE started to move back down the beach towards the Casino with the intention of returning to the promenade. An accumulation of the chert rocks broke the left track, immobilising BELLICOSE at the junction of Red and White Beaches, right beside the grounded *TLC-3*. The gunner, Trooper W. E. 'Bill' Stannard, continued firing the 6-pounder at targets on the west headland, achieving a direct hit on a tower in the process. When a message came over the radio that some boats were coming in for evacuation, Lieutenant Bennett and his crew left the tank and took shelter behind *TLC-3*. The Germans waited until the boats were full before opening fire. Many were killed. Bennett's eyes were closed up from his earlier injury by this time. Three members of his crew told him they were going out to help the wounded. During this effort Trooper Bobby Cornelssen, Bennett's driver, was killed. When ordered back to the beach to cover the withdrawal, BEEFY and BLOODY returned near the Casino. A rain of shells first hit BLOODY's turret seal so that the 6-pounder could not traverse and then the left tread finally broke, immobilising the tank in the middle of White Beach. BLUEBELL halted in the same area, as seen in this picture.

REGIMENTAL HEADQUARTERS

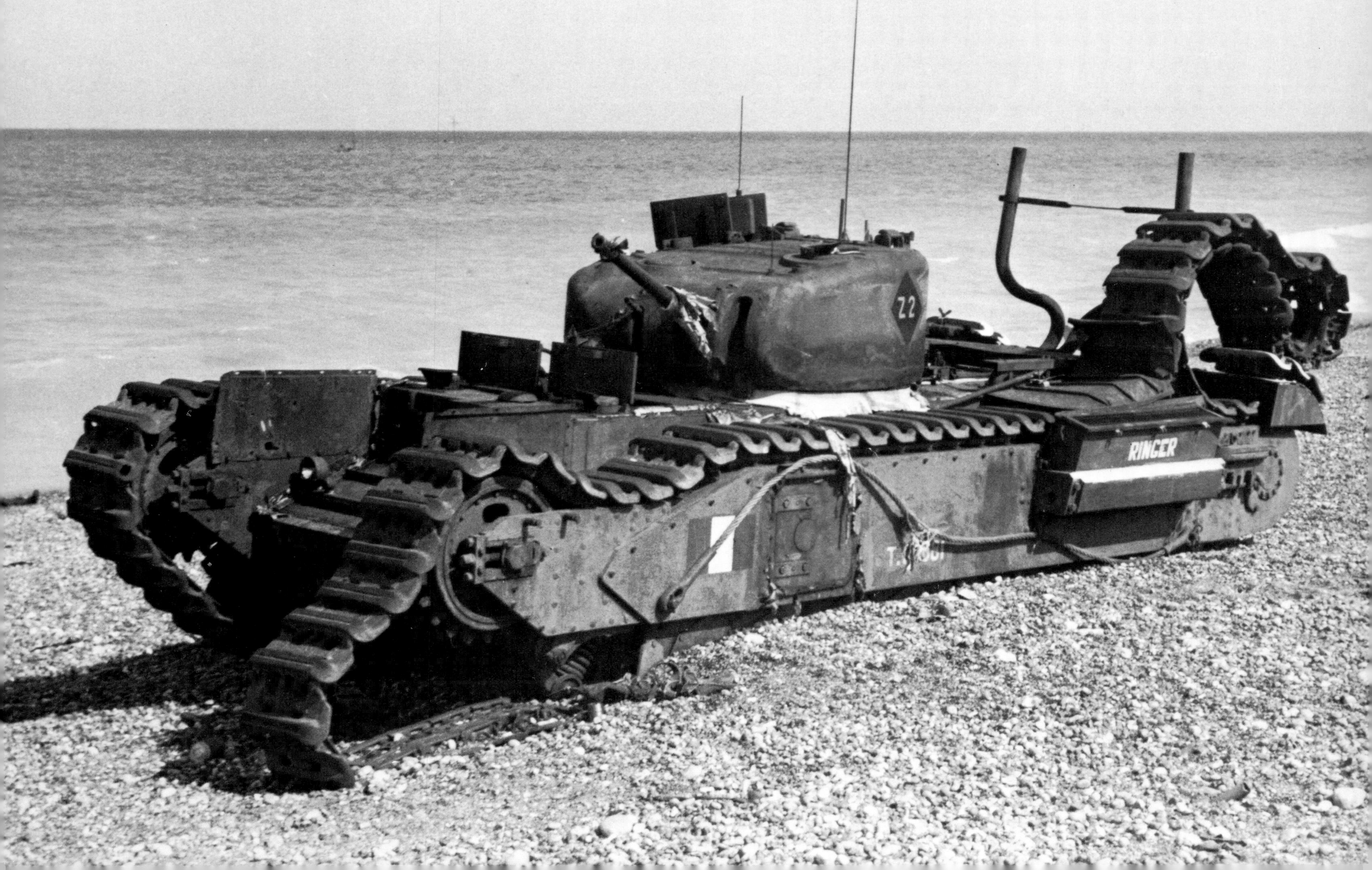

TLC-8 (No. 125) held 4th Brigade Headquarters, Brigadier Sherwood Lett, and 14 CATR Regimental Headquarters, including Lieutenant-Colonel Andrews, his second-in-command, Major John Begg, and his Adjutant, Captain Austin G. Stanton. On the first run in to Red Beach, the craft was able to land Captain Stanton in his tank RINGER [32]. Unfortunately, it was temporarily stuck in the chert, blocking the exit of the other tanks. A beach assault party of twelve sappers rushed forward carrying chespaling rolls to assist the tank. This attempt failed and seven or eight sappers were killed and their officer, Captain J. E. Bight, was twice wounded before withdrawing on board the TLC. RINGER's loader-operator, Trooper Thomas H. Pinder, recalls the action of his tank after landing: 'Almost immediately we were going up hill, very slowly, then could go no further — this was the point at which we were blocking the way of REGIMENT so the TLC had to pull out again . . . We backed down under our own power, swung to the right and started along the beach parallel to the sea in the lowest gear because of all those damnable round stones that no one mentioned beforehand. I don't remember any help from sappers to get us going. A short distance along the beach and there was a "clang" on the front of the tank and we stopped dead with at least one track broken (picture *left*). Up ahead of us we could see the Casino, and near it a large pillbox [6] which one of our tanks was bouncing 6-pounder shells off with no visible effect. There we were for the rest of the morning, using up our ammunition wherever Captain Stanton and [Trooper F. A.] Fred Tanner thought it might do some good. Every now and then a mortar shell would land on the tank, doing us no harm but creating havoc with some of the infantry who were using us for shelter . . . All through the morning the radio was a confusion of voices and orders.' When they ran out of ammunition, Captain Stanton kept his crew in the tank. As he explained: 'Nobody was getting hurt and I would not let them make a run for it because people were dying like flies on the beach. We fired up the Primus stove and had some pork and beans and bread while we waited for them to come and take us prisoner.' At some point, Lieutenant-Colonel Andrews may have gone ashore on foot to do a quick reconnaissance before returning to the TLC as it was leaving, although this is unsubstantiated. From the TLC he radioed Major Glenn, Officer Commanding C Squadron, to take command of the tanks ashore. RINGER is also seen in the picture *below* semi-submerged in the surf.

The TLC withdrew offshore for an hour or so before attempting to land its remaining two tanks on the western end of White Beach. Since no smoke cover remained, the craft attracted an extremely heavy concentration of fire. As the ramp was lowered in preparation for landing, a shell burst at the front of the landing craft, damaging the air intake louvre extensions of Colonel Andrew's tank and breaking the chains of the ramp. The ramp fell open, touching down in eight feet of water. Lieutenant-Colonel Andrews, perhaps believing a normal landing had been made, drove off and his tank, REGIMENT [2], drowned. Even at that depth he might have made the beach if the louvres and waterproofing had not been destroyed. He and the crew successfully evacuated the tank, climbing aboard a motor launch. This craft was almost immediately hit by shell-fire, bursting into flames, causing everybody to bail out. Andrews was last seen wading ashore when he was cut down by machine gun fire. His body was never found nor identified. This was a sad loss for The Calgary Regiment for he had been well liked, as a professionally trained soldier and an effective commanding officer. From 1938 to 1941 he had been part of Lieutenant-Colonel F. F. 'Fighting Frank' Worthington's Canadian Armoured Fighting Vehicle School staff at Camp Borden, Ontario. Major John Begg, in ROUNDER, was unable to land his tank because 'the volume of shell-fire increased to such an extent that TLC-8 was actually blown off the beach'. This craft withdrew with most of its crew killed, all guns out of action and having been hit by shell-fire at least 35 times. In this picture of the western end of the beach, REGIMENT can be seen in the surf on the right near the overturned LCA.

TLC-9 (No. 166) landed on White Beach soon after 0605 hours using *TLC-7* and *8* as cover on her port side. It carried 7 Troop of B Squadron, under Troop Leader Lieutenant Arthur L. 'Art' Breithaupt. BRENDA [9], under the command of Troop Sergeant W. W. 'Bill' Olive, was the first tank to land and drove immediately up the beach, blowing its waterproofing. Trooper Jim W. Horne remembers that the cordite charges did not clear all the fabric from his driver's viewport: 'As we advanced the front of the tank kept going up in the air, then dropped suddenly, hit an obstruction and killed the motor. I took this opportunity to push the port open and remove the fabric from the front. I was looking at the sea-wall on top of which was concertina wire and laying across the wire, a body [of] an engineer. I started the motor and reversed and then turned right on orders from Sergeant Olive . . . Beside the Casino was a flight of concrete steps and it was over these we made our way onto the promenade.' The co-driver of BRENDA, Trooper R. H. 'Dick' Clark, adds that: 'We had no idea we were going to land on a beach with stones the size of baseballs. There were several of us up there on the promenade . . . We were just going around in bloody circles, using up our ammo, using up our gas, being shelled, rolling over people.' Troooper Horne recounts: 'Sometime in the early afternoon we noticed two streams of smoke heading down the beach and then two planes roared by laying a smoke-screen.' BRENDA returned to the beach where the crew bailed out, Sergeant Olive burning the interior out with a sticky bomb. Later, while the crew was taking cover behind another immobilised tank nearby, they noticed BRENDA roll by into the water. Obviously, the bomb had destroyed at least the braking mechanisms.

Lieutenant Breithaupt, in BETTY [39], was the second tank off the TLC and went over the ridge into the trench. Realising that he could not cross there, Lieutenant Breithaupt backed out of the trench and then proceeded west towards the Casino. He had heard Lieutenant Bennett's announcement about the low sea-wall by the Casino. In 1945 after repatriation, Lieutenant Breithaupt officially recounted that once over the wall, BETTY and BRENDA 'spent the morning circling on the promenade clearing the infiltration of German snipers into slit trenches and firing at the buildings and cliffs from which we saw enemy fire directed to the beach. The side streets were blocked with reinforced concrete walls and were impassable by our tanks, the engineers not being able to get there to lay their charges. At about 11.15 a.m. my tank BETTY got a direct hit on the cupola which broke off the front and rear telescopes, knocked out the lights, broke off both of our aerials and knocked out both radio and inter-communication. I gave the driver instructions to drive as best he could and the gunner to fire at will, as from my position in the tank I couldn't see out or give further orders. My driver Corporal [James K.] Nash in circling noticed a large hole in which the right track was about to fall and which would have caused the tank to turn turtle. He swung the tank hard right and we went into the hole head first. When we hit the bottom right side up, the lights came on and the inter-communication and the radio started working. Corporal Nash tried to drive out of the hole, but on the crest the treads started to slip. We backed down and I called up three other tanks, Sergeant Olive [BRENDA], Sergeant Patrick [BEEFY] and Sergeant Lee [BLOODY]. Two tanks for protection from fire and one tank to tow. Corporal Nash under enemy fire attached the tow cable to Sergeant Lee's tank and we tried to get out again.' BETTY was pulled out of the hole only to have its left track shot away. Rather than go forward one track length, Lieutenant Breithaupt decided to back down into the hole to give his crew a little protection to evacuate (the 'hole' referred to by Lieutenant Breithaupt appears to have been the entrance to an underground bunker as a ventilation intake can be see in the photo *above*). His report continues: 'At this moment the order came over the air to retire to the beach and I ordered my crew into Sergeant Lee's and Sergeant Patrick's tanks, after Corporal Nash had detached the tow cable.' Three of the crew got into one and two got into the other. BEEFY's loader-operator, Trooper Raymond A. Gilbert, remembers that Trooper Harold A. Stanfield, of BETTY, was running so fast he went up over the top, onto the turret, and came down through the hatch on Trooper Gilbert's head. Lieutenant Breithaupt, after tearing off the waterproofing on the right side hatch, crawled inside, narrowly being missed by a burst of fire from a machine gun, and lay on the tool box behind the driver and co-driver (Troopers McIntyre and Lincoln). BEEFY's crew commander, Sergeant Harry R. Patrick, asked if Lieutenant Breithaupt would like to take command. He declined as they were now returning to the beach for the evacuation.

BLONDIE [36] was the last tank off the TLC towing scout car HARE [35]. It drove off and proceeded up the beach, only stopping to release HARE. While driving towards the Casino, approximately half an hour after landing, BLONDIE broke its left track and was immobilised at the western end of Red Beach. It remained there acting as a pillbox, expending all its 6-pounder and Besa ammunition before the crew abandoned it. The driver, Trooper Emil Dannewald, remembers: 'The radio got knocked out, I don't remember why, probably a mortar hit. I went out to see if I could fix my track. I could see another tank [BACKER] ahead with one track broken and nobody working on it. Then I noticed some gravel bouncing around my feet. I finally figured out what it was so I got back into the tank. The gunner [Trooper Lloyd N. Harned] said he could see them shooting from the west cliff so he concentrated fire there.' On exiting the tank, the crew picked up some weapons but, since they could not see anything to shoot at, took cover on the seaward side of the tank.

HARE [35], driven by Trooper Kasmir Doda with Corporal Chambers (RCCS), moved up the steep gradient before either being rammed by a tank manoeuvring or hit by a mortar.

The crew abandoned the area of the scout car and took cover by the sea-wall. At some point, Trooper Doda was severely wounded in the head and chest.

A Jeep [37], referred to as a 'Blitz Buggy' in contemporary documents and listed in the loading tables as belonging to 14 CATR, also landed carrying ammunition and stores. (We last saw it in England on page 3.) It was to act as an ambulance later but it never advanced very far, having difficulty on the loose stones and the driver, most probably Trooper Earl Huscroft of C Squadron Headquarters Administration, hit. It is believed that he later died of his wounds in a German hospital. The '5' is the Jeep's bridge classification.

15 TROOP, C SQUADRON

TLC-10 (No. 165), transporting 15 Troop of C Squadron, touched down at 0610 on the middle of Red Beach. The TLC also carried an engineer demolition party of 62 men under the command of Lieutenant-Colonel Barnes. In the rear of the TLC was the scout car HOUND [42] attached to the last tank and an ammunition sled that was to be hooked up, after the last tank exited, to the back of the first tank which would reverse up into the TLC. Hooking the sled was the duty of Corporal Harold L. Cooper, Headquarters Squadron. A Jeep under the command of Squadron Quartermaster Sergeant Allen Stewart, C Squadron, was to rove the beach checking on the stocks of ammunition and other supplies needed by the tanks. A total of 23 personnel from 14 CATR were on board, 15 were in the tanks, 2 were in the scout car, 1 in a Jeep, while 5 were in the ammunition party. Of the total personnel on board, only those in the tanks and scout car were able to land. *Above:* Behind CONFIDENT with its turret almost awash lies CAUSTIC.

Troop Leader Lieutenant Arthur B. Patterson was in the first tank CAUSTIC [41]. As soon as the ramp dropped the TLC was greeted with a hail of artillery and anti-tank fire, the explosions blowing water, rock splinters and shrapnel into the opening of the craft. CAUSTIC moved onto the ramp immediately after touchdown and was hit by more fire. Lieutenant Patterson, who had his head out of the turret to get a clearer view, quickly ducked inside. Contemporary reports state that the explosion stalled the tank on the ramp for a few minutes. This could have been caused by an air vacuum created by the exploding bombs close by. Having got going again, Lieutenant Patterson moved left along the beach attempting to find a way across the wide trench and sea-wall. Noticing an earth ramp going up to the height of the wall, which the Germans must have been using for their vehicles, Lieutenant Patterson drove up it.

The number two tank, CANNY [45] *(above),* followed CAUSTIC immediately but was also hit while on the ramp, receiving slight damage to its left air louvre. It turned sideways to the right and took about five minutes to straighten itself out before following after CAUSTIC. Both tanks were able to pass safely over the beach, explains Trooper Lee 'Pat' Patterson, the driver of the third tank, CONFIDENT [40], by 'turning a bit, backing up, then going ahead again, then turning a bit and so on. This defeated the piles of rubble (small rocks, bricks and pieces of concrete) that the Germans had hauled onto the beach. If the tank was turned sharply and continued ahead this rubble would pile into the tracks and go up into the drive sprockets thus snapping the tracks. The troop had picked this up on our No. 19 sets from the other troops who had landed before us and had run into this problem.' CAUSTIC and CANNY spent the morning cruising around the promenade in circles in the area of Red Beach. Lieutenant Patterson writes: 'The fire was intense and there were several tanks on this promenade . . . If at any time our tank stopped we immediately came under fire . . . We did see an enemy soldier running across the promenade — he appeared to be a dispatch runner. I ordered my gunner [Trooper Clifford J. Anderson] to get him and he did with the Besa. The word finally came over the air to pull back to the beach which we did. We went down the ramp and parked the tank . . . Lieutenant Jack Dunlap was outside the tank and asked me to attempt to silence a gun positioned near the end of the jetty, which was firing on the beach. I fired several bursts but I do not know whether I was successful or not. The beach was littered with wounded men and some disabled tanks.' CANNY also returned to the middle of Red Beach to cover the withdrawal and both crews abandoned the tanks just before the surrender.

CONFIDENT [40] had immediately followed CANNY. It had difficulties due to the longer distance it had to travel to the TLC exit, towing scout car HOUND [42] and the fact that the driver and co-driver were blinded by the waterproofing. Smoke also obscured the crew commander's vision. As CONFIDENT was going out the door it received a direct hit, fortunately a dud, above the engine compartment, causing one of the air louvres to hook the door frame and stalling the tank, half on the ramp and half on the beach. Revving its engines at the same time as the TLC reversed, the tank and scout car (which had also been hit) were released. CONFIDENT swung left to follow the other two tanks and manoeuvred over the beach in a similar manner to the others. Due to the unexpected heavy resistance and preoccupation with battle, the crew forgot about HOUND and accidentally reversed into it, ramming it into the beach (right). By now, its radios were out of action and the driver, Lance-Corporal Frank Howe, badly burned. He was the third and last man of the regiment lucky enough to be picked up off the beach and evacuated to England. (HOUND's radio operator, Corporal Wills, reported to Major Rolfe and took over the radio in HUNTER which he worked throughout the morning.) CONFIDENT climbed the ramp to the sea-wall, but was suddenly hit by concentrated shell-fire, the Germans obviously having got the range by this time. Trooper Lee Patterson describes the situation: 'There was one hell of a ringing thump and when we had collected our senses the tank had been driven back down the slope out of sight. Our steering mechanism was lying in a heap of junk where my feet should have been. I was driven back through the back of my seat into a low tool box which was behind the seat. A piece of the steering tiller was still in my hand. Trooper [Roy H.] Johnston was bleeding badly from his neck [or near one of his eyes] . . . No one was seriously hurt . . . After we got our marbles together we started the engine and drove up to the top to have a look see and fire a shot or two at whatever seemed worthwhile, then back down again before they could hit us again.' CONFIDENT used this tactic for several hours. During this period the tank gradually moved sideways to the left but after a while the gunner, Trooper James J. 'Dad' Pewtress, was not able to depress his 6-pounder low enough to shoot at anything because the tank was angled up. Since they were no longer useful, the crew evacuated, blew up the inside and took cover. Later the brakes let go and it rolled slowly backwards into the water, disappearing in a cloud of steam.

A Universal Carrier [14] of the Royal Regiment of Canada lies abandoned in front of BUTTERCUP with BLOODY on the right and BRENDA in the water. The carrier was probably under the command of Major McCool (PMLO) of the same regiment. The PMLO was the senior military authority in the beach area and therefore in charge of beach defences, movement of tanks, material and military personnel during the assault and withdrawal phases, and keeping the Headquarters' ships informed of the situation on the beaches. He worked in close conjunction with the PBM, Commander Lambert, who was the senior naval authority ashore. Their main beach headquarters was to be set up near the boundary of Red and White Beaches. Other naval and military beach signal headquarters were supposed to establish themselves separately on Red and White Beaches. The military and naval beach parties, totalling 41 and 59 men respectively, were spread throughout the LCAs and first six TLCs. The majority of them became casualties, many from snipers' bullets, soon after landing. Having no operating signals, Major McCool constantly had to run out to the exposed scout car HUNTER [38] to send messages.

WITHDRAWAL AND IMPRISONMENT

Since the whole of A Squadron and the remaining three troops of C Squadron were never sent in, and the disembarked tanks were trapped on the promenade, the two tank beach parties, instead of carrying out their planned initial tasks of directing the tanks to their objectives, spent most of their time in assisting wounded and organising tank cover for the general withdrawal.

A description of the actions of Captain Eldred, Assistant Military Landing Officer (Tank) on Red Beach, gives an idea of their activities and the chaotic situation on the beaches. Still aboard the half-beached *TLC-3* at 0600 hours, Captain Eldred could see that the beach was under intense mortar and machine gun fire pinning down the infantry. At 0615 hours Captain Turney, SAMLO(T), ordered Captain Eldred and his party ashore with instructions to order all mobile tanks off the beach because they were

Seventeen LCAs were lost during the operation, the majority in desperate attempts to evacuate men from the beaches during the last hours of the battle.

attracting heavy fire and causing unnecessary casualties among the infantry. Captain Eldred and his two men covered the 400 yards of beach unhurt by 'moving between machine gun bursts and using whatever cover was available'. He set up his post beside one of the breakwaters.

Leaving Squadron Sergeant-Major Robert Cordner and Corporal Vern Leonard at this point, Captain Eldred made a reconnaissance and counted five tanks in the centre area of Red and White beaches. Two were out of action, two started moving and firing when he signalled, and the last failed to take any action. Two scout cars in flames (HORACE and HELEN) were also in this area.

At 0645 hours, Captain Eldred noted that on Red Beach the Essex Scottish Regiment had suffered severe casualties on landing and had only been able to advance as far as the large excavated trench beside the sea-wall. Later Eldred recorded that: 'The [Essex-Scottish] second-in-command asked me to get tank support, pointing out to me the machine gun strong points and the pillboxes, which were too far away (200 to 300 yards) and surrounded by too much wire for them to get at without some tank support.' Eldred continued on his beach reconnaissance and found that the heavy German artillery and mortar concentrations made movement very difficult.

On the way back to his post, he met Commander Lambert (PBM) and Major McCool (PMLO) who had finally established their headquarters after intensive shelling had frustrated two previous attempts. By this time the only operating radio post, that in the scout car HUNTER, under the command of Major Rolfe, was constantly under enemy small arms fire. Captain Eldred noted: 'I received authority from Major McCool to leave the beach in order to secure a tank to take out the machine gun emplacements which were holding up the infantry. I passed through the wire to the promenade, found a tank, ordered it back to a position on the beach and directed the tank to fire into these posts.'

About 0715 hours, the Fusiliers Mont-Royal and the Royal Marine Commandos landed on White Beach. Eldred recounts that this caused the Germans to open up with all their weapons along the whole length of the beaches, negating any advantages gained by taking out the machine gun posts.

At 0830, Captain Eldred received instructions that the evacuation would take place as scheduled at 1000 hours. From then on, all beach parties were engaged in organising for the evacuation. Eldred recorded that: 'A second tank [CAUSTIC] by now had arrived on Red Beach and was assigned the task of engaging machine gun fortifications along the high wall and laying down a smoke-screen along the left flank. I considered that the smoke might give us some protection from the snipers who were taking a heavy toll. This tank took up a position on the beach but drew so much high explosive fire that it became necessary to clear the troops away from the area along the water line. This tank was under the command of Lieutenant Patterson, 14 CATR, and helped the infantry machine gun crews considerably in keeping down small arms fire.'

At 1000 hours, Captain Eldred concluded that the infantry was rapidly using up small arms ammunition and that the situation was critical. At 1100 hours, Major Glenn ordered all remaining mobile tanks to withdraw to the beach and take up defensive positions to cover the withdrawing infantry. It seems that the Germans were preparing for an infantry counter-attack which the tanks probably deterred. By noon all tanks had been immobilised, the majority with broken tracks, although many continued to fire until they ran out of ammunition. Contemporary reports that some tanks actually entered the back streets of the town are false. The crews were ordered to evacuate at 1225 hours. At 1300 hours, about the time of general surrender on Red and White Beaches, General Roberts sent out the code-word VANCOUVER, the signal for the entire naval force to turn around and head back to port.

59

Having left the sea-front, prisoners are marched inland along the Rue de Sygogne. Identifiable in this picture are Squadron Sergeant-Major Gerald Menzies [A] and Trooper Felix Noel [B] of BERT, Lieutenant Jack Dunlap [C] of BOB and Lieutenant Bryce Douglas [D] of CALGARY.

CONCLUSION

In review, 29 tanks attempted to land, 2 drowned and the rest made it to shore. Of these 27, 15 crossed the sea-wall, although 10 ultimately returned to the beach in the area of the Casino, where 4 were immobilised by the chert. The remaining 12 tanks never got off the beach. Of these, 4 had their tracks broken by shell-fire, 4 by the chert and 3 for uncertain reasons. The last tank stayed on the beach and was mobile for the duration of the battle.

Of the 32 officers and 392 other ranks (ORs) of the 14 CATR embarked in England, 17 officers and 154 ORs landed; of these 2 officers and 10 ORs were killed, 3 ORs were evacuated, 15 officers and 142 ORs were taken prisoner, some of them wounded, while 15 officers and 241 ORs of A Squadron, the three fighting troops of C Squadron and those remaining from B Squadron were ordered to return to England.

The raid failed because the 'Jubilee' plan was too inflexible, complicated and lacked essential heavy bombardment from sea and air. All units had precise objectives but there were no contingency plans. Another serious fault was the COHQ's neglect in using the air/ground co-operation and support structure available to it. The Army Liaison Officer attached to the Royal Air Force headquarters, Lieutenant-Colonel Charles Carrington, later wrote that there was 'nothing to be learned from Dieppe, except how not to do it, a little late in the war to learn that lesson'. This remark is also correct in reference to the raid in general. Other obvious defects were an over-reliance on surprise, which was not achieved, inadequate inter-service communications and supporting naval fire, and a lack of intelligence on the defences. These were the germs of failure as one German report concluded.

From the point of view of the 14 CATR, the major intelligence failure was not identifying the geological nature of Dieppe's chert beach, which defeated at least eight tanks, in other words, nearly one-third of those ashore. Major Sucharov's beach track-laying device attached to some of the lead tanks had not, as many historians claim, been meant to aid the tanks over this hazardous obstacle. This is obvious since the length of chespaling carried was only slightly longer than the tank itself, whereas the beach was 30-50 yards wide depending on the tide. Instead, the device was designed to give a tank traction at the moment of crossing the two-foot-high sea-wall. Two of the three tanks carrying this device successfully used it as it was designed, although one had problems jettisoning the apparatus which had either been damaged by enemy shell-fire or was technically faulty.

The success of the experimental waterproofing and deep wading attachments on the tanks cannot be determined because almost all the TLCs landed dry and many tanks received damage to their exhaust and air intake louvres and waterproofing before and while exiting the TLCs, resulting in two drowning. Most of these problems were caused either by the tanks scraping against the sides of the TLCs or by enemy fire. Better disembarking training and firing trials on the deep wading equipment might have avoided some of these difficulties.

All but two tanks successfully blew their waterproofing; in those cases it jammed the turrets and had to be cut loose. Turret jams were also caused by shell-fire hitting the turret ring, a technical problem that also could have been foreseen with more testing.

At least two scout cars were rammed by their towing tanks, probably because tank crews forgot about them in the excitement of battle and confusion caused by the

In all, 34 naval vessels were lost on the operation. Here, photographed from the West Jetty, TLC1 [48] wallows in the shallows at the eastern end of the beach.

unexpected fierce enemy resistance. Again, more training under simulated battle conditions might have avoided the problem.

The tanks were also severely undergunned, 12 having 2-pounders while the other 17 had 6-pounders, the latter not even having high explosive shells. Although some of the technical problems of the tanks could have been avoided through more testing and training (the 14 CATR had less than two months of amphibious assault training before the raid), it probably would not have made much difference to the outcome of the battle.

The objectives and orders of the 14 CATR in the raid showed the shattering ineptness of COHQ's tactical planning and the inadequacy of Allied armoured doctrine at this stage in the war. The futile decision to send tanks into a heavily fortified town was based on the outdated armoured tactics of the First World War.

To have planned a tank attack across such a steep chert beach without adequate trials on a similar beach, such as available at Dover, is, in afterthought, incomprehensible. Additionally, the idea of using tanks, with their limited gun elevation and visual capabilities, to fight through a major built-up area, without considerable support, indicates gross ignorance or deliberate overlooking of the operational limitations of tanks. Only one sniper's bullet is necessary to kill a tank commander who tries to improve vision by putting his head outside the turret.

The plan is astonishing when it is recalled that the 14 CATR had been trained for infantry support either in the open countryside or on the sandy beaches of the Isle of Wight. The regiment never had any training in the complex and dangerous type of close-quarter house to house fighting, necessitating extremely close infantry co-operation, that it would have encountered if its tanks had been able to penetrate the narrow streets.

Immediately after the Dieppe Raid, the people responsible for its inception and planning, namely COHQ and Admiral Mountbatten, justified the huge losses in men and material by claiming that the 'lessons learned' would lead to future victory and a saving of lives when the final invasion of Fortress Europe took place. The COHQ report stated that the need for heavy supporting fire was the most important lesson learned from the Dieppe raid. Similarly, German reports reveal that the Germans were surprised that such an attack was attempted without the required supporting fire. The successful Normandy landings in 1944 strengthened this argument but this certainly was not a new lesson, especially after the experiences of the Great War and specifically the disastrous amphibious landing at Gallipoli.

In the post-war decades, military historians have questioned the necessity of the raid and particularly the selection of Dieppe as a target and the choice of tactics used. The official Canadian army historian explains that: 'Surprise, rather than striking power, was the chief reliance in this operation; yet no surprise could be hoped for in the frontal attack, which was to go in half an hour later than those on the flanks . . . It seems impossible to avoid the conclusion that from the beginning the planners underrated the influence of topography and of the enemy's strong defences in the Dieppe area.'

Of the twelve 14 CATR officers and men who lost their lives on the raid, seven are buried in the Dieppe War Cemetery: Captain Douglas Purdy (Row A Grave 23), Sergeant-Major Alexander Tough of the White Beach Party (Row L Grave 20), with Troopers Robert Cornelssen (Row E Grave 52), Peter Friesen (Row L Grave 66), Thomas Gorman (Row F Grave 11), Victor Olliffe (Row K Grave 63) and Charles Provis (Row A Grave 57). The body of Lieutenant-Colonel Johnny Andrews was never recovered and he is now commemorated on Panel 23 of Column 2 at the Brookwood Memorial to the Missing at Brookwood, Surrey. Trooper Earl Huscroft is believed to have died of wounds in a German hospital but his grave has never been found. He is also commemorated at Brookwood on Panel 23. Trooper William Stewart, last seen swimming out to sea, is buried in Boulogne Eastern Cemetery (Plot 12, Row E, Grave 20) and Trooper Michael Zima is in Calais Canadian War Cemetery (Plot 8, Row F, Grave 4). Corporal Dwight Earl Welch of the White Beach Party died of wounds on August 31, 1942 and is now buried in Grave 10 of Row D in Plot 4 of the Holten Canadian War Cemetery (12 miles east of Deventer) in the Netherlands. Meanwhile, at Dieppe, the battle over, the clear-up continues with the equipment of the regiment being recovered, repaired and put back into service . . . under new masters.

It is not true that important new strategic lessons were learned since none were unknown beforehand. More appropriate is it to say that they were relearned. The claim that the idea of logistical support through open beaches, and the use of prefabricated Mulberry harbours, were a direct result of the raid are false. Contemporary records reveal that, even after the operation, COHQ planners remained 'port conscious'. Acquisition of a port intact remained an unchangeable determinant in all invasion planning, except that the emphasis changed to the best way of doing so by means of envelopment. It was only after the Sicilian landings that the idea of beach maintenance started to take hold.

Tactical lessons are learned in every battle and some were learned at Dieppe. Unfortunately, all the men most qualified to fill out the after-action reports concerning the tanks' performance during the operation, namely the tank crews themselves, were PoWs. Of the three 14 CATR men that returned, only Trooper Volk made a report. During the remainder of the war only three more were received: from Major Page, Lieutenent Bennett and Corporal Thomas L. Carnie on their repatriation.

Since the Normandy landings, historians and participants, in efforts to justify the huge casualties, have tended to over-exaggerate these tactical lessons. They have given undue credit to the raid for the development and subsequent use of ideas at Normandy, most of which were already under development prior to Dieppe. The most obvious example is the constant reference to the successful use of the 'Funnies' — specialised armoured assault vehicles. However, experimentation with these types of vehicles had been under way before the raid, and as early as the Great War.

The experience necessary for the major invasion of the Continent could have been gained far more easily and with far less casualties from the amphibious landings on Sicily, the Italian mainland, North Africa and the Japanese-held Pacific islands.

Notwithstanding all of the foregoing comments, it is fitting to pay tribute to the naval, army and air personnel who attempted to carry out their allotted tasks. The courageous action of The Calgary Regiment's tank crews in providing covering fire to help the few infantry and other survivors to evacuate Dieppe beach explains why all except three of the men were taken prisoner. These valiant men fought until all their ammunition had been used up, by which time they had to choose between death or imprisonment. It was a painful yet obvious choice and a sad ending to the worst defeat in Canadian military history.

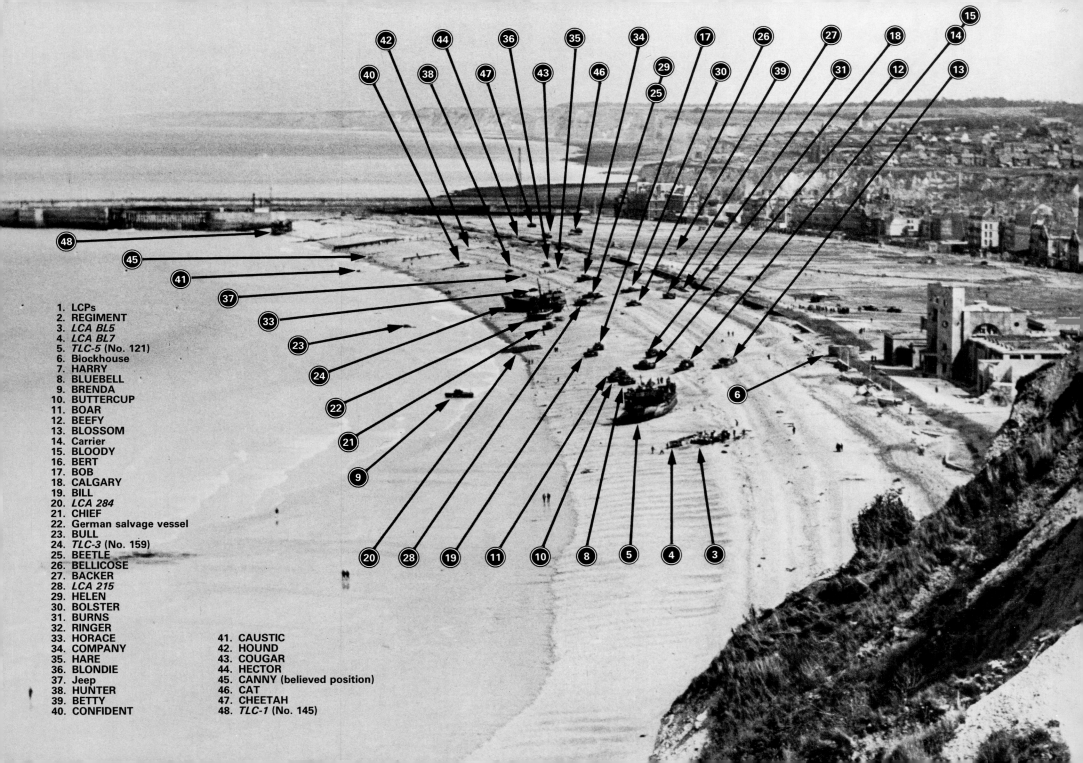

1. LCPs
2. REGIMENT
3. *LCA BL5*
4. *LCA BL7*
5. *TLC-5* (No. 121)
6. Blockhouse
7. HARRY
8. BLUEBELL
9. BRENDA
10. BUTTERCUP
11. BOAR
12. BEEFY
13. BLOSSOM
14. Carrier
15. BLOODY
16. BERT
17. BOB
18. CALGARY
19. BILL
20. *LCA 284*
21. CHIEF
22. German salvage vessel
23. BULL
24. *TLC-3* (No. 159)
25. BEETLE
26. BELLICOSE
27. BACKER
28. *LCA 215*
29. HELEN
30. BOLSTER
31. BURNS
32. RINGER
33. HORACE
34. COMPANY
35. HARE
36. BLONDIE
37. Jeep
38. HUNTER
39. BETTY
40. CONFIDENT
41. CAUSTIC
42. HOUND
43. COUGAR
44. HECTOR
45. CANNY (believed position)
46. CAT
47. CHEETAH
48. *TLC-1* (No. 145)